They Still Can't Spell?
Understanding and Supporting Challenged Spellers in Middle and High School

Rebecca Bowers Sipe

with
Dawn Putnam, Karen Reed-Nordwall,
Tracy Rosewarne, Jennifer Walsh

Foreword by Kylene Beers

HEINEMANN
Portsmouth, NH

Heinemann
A division of Reed Elsevier Inc.
361 Hanover Street
Portsmouth, NH 03801–3912
www.heinemann.com

Offices and agents throughout the world

The author and publisher wish to thank those who have generously given permission to reprint borrowed material:

"Candidate for a Pullet Surprise" by Dr. Jerrold Zar in *The Journal of Irreproducible Results*, January/February 1994. Reprinted by permission of the author and Wisdom Simulators, Inc., Cambridge, Massachusetts.

Library of Congress Cataloging-in-Publication Data
Sipe, Rebecca Bowers.
    They still can't spell? : understanding and supporting challenged
spellers in middle and high school / Rebecca Bowers Sipe with Jennifer Walsh . . . [et al.] ;
foreword by Kylene Beers.
        p.   cm.
    Includes bibliographical references and index.
    ISBN 0-325-00539-7 (alk. paper)
    1. English language—Orthography and spelling—Study and teaching (Middle school)—
United States—Case studies.   2. English language—Orthography and spelling—Study
and teaching (Secondary)—United States—Case studies.   I. Title.
LB1574.S53 2003
428.1—dc21   2003006681

Editor: James Strickland
Production: Vicki Kasabian
Cover design: Night & Day Design
Typesetter: TechBooks
Manufacturing: Steve Bernier

Printed in the United States of America on acid-free paper
07   06   05   04   03   RRD   1   2   3   4   5

For their willingness to be a part of my world of questions,
this book is dedicated to
Tracy, Jennifer, Karen, and Dawn and their wonderful families,
my husband, Michael,
Dera and Justin,
the many students who informed our work,
and
Robert Bowers—my dad—who should still be here to celebrate with me.

Contents

Contents

Foreword

"So, when you grade this, are you going to count off for spelling?"

I looked at the student standing at my desk, about to turn in her assignment. Since this student was thirty-something, was working on a master's degree in reading, and had been a teacher for eight years, I wondered, for a moment, if she was simply repeating a question that she surely had heard many times in her own teaching career. But something in her face, something in the tone of her question, let me know this question was hers. I answered her question with a question: "Why would you ask that?" She shrugged, frowned, waited, and finally responded, "I'm not a good speller. I mean I am really not a good speller. I think I caught all my mistakes, but my husband, who usually reads all my papers, is out of town."

I asked another question: "Do you count off when your middle schoolers make spelling mistakes?" No pause this time. "No. I mean, maybe I should, but I know what it feels like when you can't spell. All through my own school years teachers counted off and that never helped me become a better speller. Not once. It just helped me learn to use shorter, easier words. One teacher got so angry with me one year, she counted off 10 points every time I misspelled a word. One paper, I got something like a negative 80. I never understood why she thought counting off all those points would make me a better speller. Did she think I could spell better just by wanting to? If wanting was all it took, I'd have been the national spelling bee champion from about fourth grade on."

"So, when your students misspell words, what do you do that you think helps them?" I asked, pushing away the memory of the times I had taken off points when my own middle school students had misspelled words.

"Well, I *give* students points every time they spell words correctly that they have previously misspelled. So, like Matt, last week, he made a 150 on something he turned in because he spelled so many words correctly. You should have seen his grin. It was great. You know, kids say to me all the time, 'Does spelling count?' and I tell them that 'Yes, in this class spelling counts, it just doesn't count *off*.' Beyond that, I don't know. We just work on spelling all the time, you know? I don't really know what to do. I wish someone would write a book on how teachers can help older kids with spelling."

Sometimes wishes come true. After four years of solid research on the spelling habits of adolescents, Becky Sipe and her research team of four teachers have written the book that many of us have wanted for a long time. If you never imagined yourself reaching for a book on teaching spelling, think again. Set against the backdrop of four different classrooms, *They Still Can't Spell?* is as interesting as it is instructive. Filled with student comments, this book offers you a chance to hear what adolescents who struggle with spelling think of themselves as readers, as writers, as thinkers. On page 2, you'll meet Kevin, a teacher who offers a view that many secondary teachers hold: "The thing . . . about spelling is that it's just so trivial." But then almost immediately you meet Justin, a challenged speller, who points out that "it's only trivial to people who know how to do it."

While I don't have any statistics in front of me, my hunch is that most secondary English teachers are good spellers. For those teachers, spelling *is* trivial. But Justin's comment changes everything. It is *only* trivial if you can do it. Think about tying your shoelaces: a trivial thing that you've been able to do for decades. Now be three-years-old. Suddenly figuring out how to tie your shoelaces is entrée into a bit of independence, a move into the big kids' world, not trivial at all. Throughout this book, Becky constantly brings us back into the world of students like Justin with student work, vignettes, and interviews. Their words keep the book fascinating; her analysis of their comments keeps the reading compelling.

Becky uses the individual voices of specific students to create templates of spellers; these templates, in turn, provide an instructional map for teaching struggling spellers. These templates, or what Becky calls profiles, outline different types of challenged spellers, thus showing us that all struggling spellers are not alike. With these profiles, you suddenly understand why some students who are challenged spellers still love to write (for them, spelling is an editing issue and is not what identifies someone as a good or poor writer) while other challenged spellers hate to write (for them, writing is spelling and thus being a weak speller means being a weak writer). The insight that Becky provides on students' perception of self as a speller, ability to self-correct, visual memory, and depth and breadth of spelling strategies forges new ground in our understanding of struggling spellers and their problems. But she doesn't stop there. She also explains to readers how to analyze the types of spelling errors students make and then shows us how specific strategies help correct certain errors.

The result: a book that gives teachers insight into challenged spellers, that helps teachers understand how to teach spelling in a powerful way, and that moves dependent spellers toward independence. *They Still Can't Spell?* moves to the forefront something that, when taught correctly, can then move to the background of students' knowledge. In other words, she shows us all the right ways to make spelling count.

Kylene Beers
Editor, *Voices from the Middle*
Author, *When Kids Can't Read*
Senior Reading Researcher
School Development Program
Yale University

Preface

We've all worked with challenged spellers. Some of us *are* challenged spellers. In each case, one thing is certain: difficulties with spelling can be frustrating and embarrassing, potentially causing those who struggle to avoid tasks that produce these feelings—tasks like writing. Despite the fact that spelling is such a small part of the writing process, it becomes disproportionately significant in academic, social, and business settings. For many, difficulties with spelling translate to an invisible handicap that is carefully hidden and that may affect routine daily tasks. As teachers and parents, we are all too aware of judgments about a writer's education, intelligence, or background that are made simply because she spells words incorrectly. We know students are often penalized because of spelling "carelessness" in schoolwork and job applications are often cast aside because of spelling errors.

Those who have never struggled with spelling may underestimate the challenges poor spellers face and harbor oversimplified notions about how to address such problems. Across the country we now observe a wave of concern at the middle and high school levels about the marginal spelling abilities of many students. As teachers, administrators, and parents have become alarmed, there is a renewed interest in providing assistance to adolescents and young adults who flounder when trying to spell even routine, high-use words.

As teachers, we desperately want to help these young people gain skill with spelling because we know poor spelling will affect their success in school and in work settings. Unfortunately, our good intentions are hampered by several complications. First, most of us who teach at the middle and high school level were never taught how to teach spelling. Though we may have had coursework in linguistics and in writing methods, we may have only our own memories of learning to spell to draw upon to help shape our spelling instruction. Second, because most research on spelling has focused on younger learners and their development into competent spellers, we may not understand the kinds of problems that secondary students have with spelling. As a result, our best efforts to support challenged spellers may simply replicate methods that weren't successful in the first place—a circumstance virtually guaranteed to frustrate our students and us.

Dawn, Jennifer, Karen, Tracy, and I, all colleagues in the Eastern Michigan Writing Project (a local affiliate of the National Writing Project), share both a belief that spelling is a writing skill best addressed in final draft writing and a concern about the spelling struggles of our middle school, high school, and college students. We created a teacher research group to investigate their dilemmas because we wanted to know more about what they were facing, the specific strengths and weaknesses that created their platforms for spelling, and the types of experiences with spelling that had supported or interfered with their growth. Moreover, we wanted to identify or create new strategies to use now—in middle and high school settings—to help these students gain better control of their spelling and to help level the playing field by building their confidence and competence in writing and spelling.

To pursue these goals, we developed a collaborative study in which student informants participated as coresearchers with us, helping us to compile individual case studies. To accommodate the many voices we needed, our study included classroom observations, analyses of first and final draft student writing, transcripts of multiple face-to-face interviews, spelling placement inventories, short- and long-term visual memory inventories, and researcher observations. After a full academic year of collecting data, distinct descriptive categories of challenged spellers began to emerge. We began to see patterns in background instructional experiences and overall literacy investment. From this enormous amount of information, we were able to explore and catalog the types of strategies that appeared most beneficial to address the needs of these various types of challenged spellers.

This book is a story of our findings and what those findings suggest for instruction in our classrooms. In Part 1 we offer concise profiles of the four categories of challenged spellers and share some core understandings about the types of strategies and approaches challenged spellers need to support their development. In Part 2 we describe and translate these core understandings into classroom strategies. In Part 3 our teacher researchers offer glimpses into their classrooms as they put our strategies into practice. The classrooms each share common features that help to promote a positive environment for spelling growth as well as reflect some distinct differences. These classrooms show how teachers modified their application of our findings to fit the needs of their students and their own curricular restraints. In Part 4 we explore issues teachers will need to consider as they contemplate changes at the classroom, school, and district level. In Part 5, we discuss how to look for evidence that will prove your new spelling instruction is working.

Finally, in Part 6 we provide a catalog of strategies, activities, and materials for immediate use in the classroom.

Most of all, we attempt to place a human frame around the dilemmas faced by adolescent challenged spellers. Throughout these pages, we weave in stories of student writers and attempt to situate this discussion in the context of both their writing lives and the reality of secondary teaching. After all, spelling is a writing skill. If the practices we use to teach spelling do not translate into better writing, then why bother? If the strategies we identify can't be woven into real classrooms, how can they help?

Acknowledgments

This book and the questions that prompted it belong to many people. From my earliest years of reading and writing, I knew that spelling mattered—and I knew that I struggled with it. I knew that my dad was a challenged speller also, so whatever was wrong with me was wrong with him, too. Life was unfair that way, and that was that. I was highly invested in literacy, so I developed lots of ways to keep my spelling struggles to myself.

Years later, as I began my teaching career working with wonderfully talented seventh and eighth graders, I revisited my frustrations with spelling through the struggles of my students. In desperation, I sought out spelling texts, tried every strategy I could think of, and watched helplessly as they continued to struggle.

My questions about spelling took a giant leap forward as I watched my own two bright and articulate children and the child of a dear friend grow as readers and writers. These young people taught me much about literacy development and about the reasons many conventional approaches used to teach spelling fail to work for some children. It was they who helped me begin to understand the importance of my questions about spelling and spelling instruction.

Along the way I have been fortunate to work with colleagues like Kathy Short, Dan Kirby, Marilyn Buckley, Jane Evanson, and Elaine Snowden, who have taken an interest in my questions and encouraged my pursuit of them. I have been doubly blessed to have Dera Mabry as a grandmother. Even at the age of eighty-eight, she reminds me frequently that I can accomplish anything if I keep asking questions. And, of course, I have my new colleagues in Michigan, without whom this book might never have been written.

Let me tell you about four amazing teachers. Jennifer Walsh, Dawn Putnam, Karen Reed-Nordwall, and Tracy Rosewarne change the lives of adolescents every day. Each of these teachers shared my concerns and questions about challenged spellers. Each opened up classrooms and spent enormous amounts of personal time as we engaged in this four-year effort. This book is dedicated to them, to their families, and to their students just as it is to my father, husband, children, and students at Eastern Michigan.

I would like to acknowledge the gracious gifts of time and response given to me by Kylene Beers and Kathleen Rowlands. Their careful critique and welcomed encouragement have been blessings. In addition, both the National Council of Teachers of English and Eastern Michigan University have supported my work with research funding, for which I am much in their debt.

Finally, I know I would never have had the confidence to complete this project if it were not for my wonderful friend and editor, Jim Strickland. He brought to this project a rare blend of patience, encouragement, and blue ink. He's taught me so much, and I am indeed grateful.

I

Who Are Challenged Spellers?

I know they think I'm stupid but I'm not. I'm good at lots of things. I just can't spell. Even when I study, I can't guarantee the words will come when I need them.

JON

1

Investigating Challenged Spellers

The thing I think about spelling is that it's just so trivial.
—Kevin, a teacher

Kevin's response gave me pause. I couldn't argue with his statement. In the grand scheme of things, spelling does seem trivial. My fellow teacher researchers and I believe that spelling is a writing skill best addressed in final draft writing. Yet, within the frame of this belief, my many conversations with challenged spellers had convinced me that spelling was anything but trivial. For people who struggle with spelling, it sometimes takes on far greater significance than it otherwise would.

As so often has been the case, it was my son who helped frame my thinking. Justin is a challenged speller whose difficulties with spelling were identified early. With the assistance of many fine teachers, Justin is a capable writer and university student today. However, he is still a challenged speller. When I repeated Kevin's comment about spelling being trivial, Justin replied, "Yeah, Mom . . . but it's only trivial to people who know how to do it. . . ."

For Justin, spelling has never been trivial. Over the years he helped me understand that the phenomenon I labeled "challenges with spelling" has many dimensions. Despite Justin's spelling difficulties, his writing, when composed at a keyboard, was typically coherent and thoughtful, reflecting strong voice, organization, and interesting ideas. For the most part, punctuation and capitalization were used correctly. He often experimented to create a desired effect in his stories. In first draft writing, however, few readers ever got beyond his chaotic spelling.

Years earlier I remember finding a note on his desk from a girl in his middle school class. "Have you written her back?" I asked him at the time. With a steadfast look he replied, "I don't write. . . ." Justin's gaze had told the full story: *I don't write anything if I stand a chance of being embarrassed.* In middle school, Justin's two major strategies for correct spelling were spell checkers and Mom . . . neither of which would serve him well for writing a note to a girl. His concern about spelling, and the embarrassment that poor spelling could bring, inhibited his ability to write notes or handwritten letters to friends or to engage in routine writing activities that most of us take for granted.

For years I had encouraged my students to postpone their concerns about spelling until their final drafts. "Don't sweat the small stuff!" I'd cajole. "Wait until it's time to clean up the 'sloppy copy.'" It was Justin who initially helped me see things in a different light. For Justin—and other writers like him—spelling is far more than just "small stuff." Spelling presents a major obstacle to writing every time he sits down to compose. Even though he is a proficient young adult writer, his spelling often adheres to strict phonetic principles. With a certainty, writing completed under pressure and without adequate tools creates a recipe for failure. Under such circumstances, it is not uncommon for him to spell many words incorrectly.

As is often the case with challenged spellers, classmates and teachers may have generalized several assumptions from this dismal performance over the years (Gentry 1987): Justin can't spell, so he can't write; Justin can't spell, so he isn't smart; Justin can't spell, so he isn't dedicated or motivated or concerned about his work; Justin can't spell, so he must be lazy. Sadly, Justin may have unconsciously bought in to some of these generalizations as well, a possibility demonstrated by his efforts to limit his engagement with handwritten texts.

Just as those inexperienced with spelling challenges may oversimplify how to address spelling problems, they may also underestimate the numbers of challenged spellers in their classrooms. As many as one out of every five adults in the United States experiences significant difficulty with spelling, according to some estimates, including "closet poor spellers," or adults who struggle with spelling and who, for a variety of reasons, fear others finding out about their problem (Kelly 1992). Like Justin, Nancy, a middle school student, helped me see the weight and significance a challenged speller may place on spelling when she wrote: "I think it [spelling] is important because spelling counts on your papers. You can't get a good job and *proboly* not *grauate* from high school. I feel *dum* because when people read my paper they have to ask me what the word is." While attitudes about spelling are reinforced in school, Nancy reminds us that many students attach values to spelling that reach far beyond the school setting (see Figure 1–1). She perceived spelling as limiting her ability to succeed in school and in the workplace. Clearly, for Nancy, poor spelling led to feelings of inadequacy and inability.

Poor spellers

- are lazy.
- don't care about their work.
- aren't as intelligent as other folks.
- can't write.
- won't be successful in school.

Figure 1–1. Common Fallacies About Poor Spellers

Parents also have a strong role in shaping students' attitudes about spelling. Dan, a tenth grader, for example, resists his mother's association between poor spelling and weak thinking. He writes,

> my mom really has a big thing about it [spelling]. If I don't get it correct, she makes me write it over. She *things* that spelling actually *ahs* something to do with mental stuff . . . that you're actually thinking a lot better if you know how to spell. But, I don't *tink* that's really true because, honestly, for me, I think all the time . . . I just like math classes. I get like high grades. My science class, I get high grades, and still I have a problem writing sometimes.

Certainly, many of Dan's spelling errors could be perceived by others as the result of weak proofreading. Unfortunately, not all students possess Dan's clear sense of competency in areas of strength.

Equally misleading are fallacious notions of what challenged spellers need. Misguided suggestions include more phonics, heavier use of spelling texts, stronger emphasis on tests, and attaching greater penalties for spelling errors found in written work. These notions tend to be far too simplistic to address the types of problems challenged spellers actually face, as we will discuss later in the student case studies.

Some may even argue that technology makes concerns about spelling moot, but this is clearly not the case. While tools like spell checkers have helped many of us experience a more level playing field, there is no substitute for reaching a level of automaticity with high-use words, thus freeing the writer to concentrate on the creation of meaning rather than the construction of language. Because a spell checker picks up only incorrectly spelled words, homophones and other word substitutions may slip through easily. Without strong proofreading skills, one can quickly find herself in an embarrassing situation as wrong words take meaning in radically unintended directions! A poem by Jerry Zar (1994) provides a delightful illustration (Figure 1–2). By the author's count, 127 of the 225 words of the poem are incorrect, although all the words are spelled correctly. While spell checkers are helpful tools, only knowledge of spelling will help students navigate the intricacies and complexities of the language and avoid embarrassing problems caused by faulty proofreading (Strickland 1997, 71–73).

The point is, to those who do not struggle with spelling, who have never struggled with spelling, and who have been able to reserve concerns about spelling for the final draft of their writing, the huge and varied issues faced by challenged spellers are completely invisible. The students in our study helped us open our eyes to these obstacles and to new questions. How does poor spelling affect an individual's sense of self as a writer? As an intelligent person? How do these internalized beliefs affect the decisions they make—consciously and unconsciously—about

Candidate for a Pullet Surprise

I have a spelling checker
It came with my PC.
It plane lee marks four my revue
Miss steaks aye can knot sea.

Eye ran this poem threw it,
Your sure reel glad two no.
Its vary polished in it's weigh
My checker tolled me sew.

My checker is a bless sing,
It freeze yew lodes of thyme.
It helps me right awl stiles two reed,
And aides me when aye rime.

Each frays come posed up on my screen
Eye trussed too bee a joule.
The checker pour o'er every word
To cheque sum spelling rule.

Be fore a veiling checkers
Hours spelling mite decline,
And if we're lacks or have a laps,
We wood be maid too wine.

Butt now bee cause my spelling
Is checked with such grate flare,
There are know fault's with in my cite,
Of non eye am a ware.

Now spelling does knot phase me,
It does not bring a tier.
My pay purrs awl due glad den
With wrapped words fare as hear.

To rite with care is quite a feet
Of witch won should be proud.
And wee mussed dew the best wee can,
Sew flaws are knot aloud.

Sow ewe can sea why aye dew prays
Such soft ware four pea seas.
And why I brake in two averse
By righting want to pleas.

Figure 1–2. Poem by Jerry Zar

engagement with literacy? About the type of experiences they allow themselves to explore? About the academic and career choices they make? And, how do an individual's feelings of personal control over reading, over writing, and over spelling relate to each other?

While spelling may be merely a nuisance that interferes with writing for some, spelling evokes such a sense of hopelessness for others that gaining control of it may seem impossible. For some individuals, lack of competency in spelling may be a substantial obstacle to writing and may limit opportunities and access in school and beyond. Clearly, challenges with spelling may translate to an invisible handicap that is carefully hidden and that may affect many routine daily tasks.

Many voices—representing middle school through college-level writers—echoed a range of personal concerns about spelling instruction and helped shape our questions. For example, students like Rita and Lori help frame the range of struggles affecting challenged spellers. Rita, a high school student, writes that people make spelling errors because "they are *cairless*" and that she misspells words because "[she's] stupid and never *caired* to learn *acualy* [she] just can't remember." Rita's lack of ability as a speller has spilled over to distort her views of herself as capable and intelligent.

On the other hand, Lori, also a high schooler, writes, "I don't worry about spelling when I *right* because I always spell words *write*." For Lori, spelling really isn't a problem! Despite her errors, she views spelling as small stuff and spends little time fretting about it. Nonetheless, her errors affect her success in school writing and, because of societal expectations surrounding spelling, may influence her in other high-stakes writing situations beyond school.

Our inquiry was grounded in the belief that if we were to understand the scope of, causes of, and unique dilemmas posed by spelling difficulties, we had to listen to the literacy histories of challenged spellers themselves.

Learning from the Available Research

Despite Benjamin Franklin's notion that an educated person should be able to spell any word at least six different ways, the twenty-first century has found us a nation obsessed with spelling. Today, even presidential candidates may become the butt of jokes if they flounder on the spelling of a word like *potato* before a class of schoolchildren.

As secondary and college teachers, we know the frustration that results from receiving papers from challenged spellers littered with errors. Yet, as much as we would love to help them learn to spell, we are charged with teaching them American literature, tenth-grade composition, or some other tightly packed curriculum. Our situation is further complicated by the fact that most of us were never taught how to teach spelling. In fact, our exposure to spelling instruction may have ceased with our own elementary school experiences.

As secondary and college teachers, some of us are challenged spellers. As our teacher research group came together for the first time, we shared snippets of our own spelling histories. Whereas Jennifer recalled the *one* word she could remember misspelling in elementary school, I recounted the excruciating knot in my stomach I felt each week before the spelling test started and the frequent Fridays my mom had to put Band-Aids on fingers where I'd bitten them until they bled.

As we talked, Jennifer and I discovered we also had many experiences in common. Both of us had weekly lists and exercises that came from a spelling book. Both of our moms coached us, posting the word list on the refrigerator door each week and quizzing us several times during the week. We each had practice tests at school and cumulative tests that covered words from several weeks, and we received spelling grades based on the tests we took. Jennifer became a confident speller, while I, though not a bad speller, had lots of difficulty remembering words—particularly under pressure. Too often I found myself unable to visualize words, and my fear of being ridiculed and looking stupid created a powerful memory.

We came to realize that identical strategies for teaching spelling had produced very different results for us—both affectively and cognitively. Jennifer and I represented opposite ends of the spectrum, Karen, Dawn, and Tracy the middle. Spelling was never a big deal to any of them, though all three recalled particular types of words that gave them pause. We realized that each of us had acquired multiple strategies for spelling. And, though our sense of ease with spelling varied, we each placed high value on writing.

As we thought about our own experiences and shared observations about the challenged spellers in our classrooms, we found ourselves with a huge assortment of questions. What had others found about effective strategies for teaching spelling? Were there identified interferences that others had already charted and from which we could identify effective approaches? These questions pushed us toward the rich body of research already available on spelling instruction.

Interestingly, though spelling is a small piece of the overall process of writing, it has been one of the most researched areas in our discipline (Fitzsimmons and Loomer 1977). Much of the research on spelling has sought to identify strategies used by successful spellers and to understand the developmental nature of spelling acquisition in young learners. Teaching practices that were developed from these studies—like the pretest, instruction, posttest methodology, and weekly word lists (Gates 1931; Hawley and Gallup 1922)—continue to be prevalent in spelling texts today and reflect a desire to acquaint all students with the strategies and behaviors used by strong spellers.

Early in the twentieth century, refined lists of high-frequency words were developed and teachers were encouraged to use them in elementary spelling instruction (Horn 1926; Horn and Otto 1954). These high-frequency word lists have remained remarkably stable across the decades. The logic of concentrating instructional time on high-frequency words that students actually use in their writing has encouraged the development of programs with that focus (for example, see Sitton 1995).

More recent studies articulate predictable stages in spelling development, establish a clear relationship between spelling and other language processes, and encourage a more naturalistic, process approach to spelling instruction, one which advocates learning to spell words within the context of writing (Henderson 1990; Goodman 1993; Gentry and Gillet 1993; Laminack and Wood 1996; Bean and Bouffler 1997; Hughes and Searle 1997).

Five stages in spelling growth are well documented as learners progress from sound-letter relationships to ultimate competence with written words (Reed 1971; Henderson and Beers 1980; Gentry 1982; Henderson and Templeton 1986;

I: Emergent
II: Letter name–alphabetic
III: Within-word pattern
IV: Syllables and affixes
V: Derivational relations

(Bear et al. 2000)

Figure 1–3. Five Stages of Spelling Growth

Henderson 1990; Hughes and Searle 1997). As young spellers grow and mature, they continually apply and refine their knowledge of spelling conventions (Hughes and Searle 1997).

As emergent readers and writers, children in the first stage of spelling growth (see Figure 1–3) approximate letters with pictures or scribbles with no relationship to sound. The children learn letters, particularly those in their names, and will use these letters for a variety of purposes. As children move to Stage II, name-alphabetic relationship, they begin to associate sound and letters, first using only the first consonant sounds, then first and last consonants, and finally first and last consonants with a vowel sound.

During Stage III, the within-word pattern stage, children exhibit increased language fluency, moving to a recognition of chunks of letters as meaning units. It is during this stage that most children come to realize that our twenty-six letters in the alphabet do not account for all the sounds we need to represent and that multiple-letter combinations are required to produce some sounds. According to Bear et al. (2000), children in this stage possess reading vocabularies of between two hundred and four hundred words. It is during this crucial stage of literacy development that recognition of consonant-vowel patterns begins.

As children move to Stages IV and V, they reflect the behavior of fluent readers, moving beyond needing to read word by word to developing an emphasis on meaning. During Stage IV, the syllables and affixes stage, the study of language focuses on *junctures* where syllables come together, including syllables within a word and the addition of prefixes or suffixes (Bear 2000, 24). Finally, during Stage V, students are ready for language study that includes word origins and bases. Since the publication of *Syntactic Structures* (Chomsky 1957), linguists have supported the notion that language study requires reference to the underlying logic in the language. Studies of high-achieving middle and high school students suggest the need for instruction in deeper language structures and word awareness to enhance spelling accuracy (Templeton 1983).

Seeking Our Own Answers

Despite evidence that spelling is learned in predictable stages, some children fail to progress as expected. As early as first or second grade, a small identifiable group of children fails to move forward toward spelling competence. Children in this group appear unable to draw upon the more advanced strategies for spelling, such as breaking words into meaning-based units, drawing upon spelling rules, or relating words in word families (Gentry 1982; Hughes and Searle 1997). As interesting as the research was, we became aware of how much more we still needed to know about our challenged spellers, and we found ourselves returning to questions about our students' spelling histories. In what types of language study had they engaged? What strategies did they have to draw upon? Was it possible that they had not been taught—or had not sufficiently learned—the strategies necessary to help them sense how words were constructed? Was it possible for us to help them improve within our instructional settings and at this stage in their academic careers?

We adopted a very straightforward approach. We began collecting and analyzing first draft writing in which our student collaborators discussed their spelling histories. From the analysis of these papers, we constructed interview questions that helped us probe deeper into areas of interest. We asked students to take spelling placement and visual memory inventories so that we could weigh these factors in the balance. We analyzed other first and final draft pieces of writing to catalog and study the types of error patterns we found. What we discovered helped us think about how we approach language study within the total context of our teaching.

2

Getting Started
Learning from Student Spelling Histories

We extended an invitation to challenged spellers in our classes: "I'm looking for a few folks who think of themselves as challenged spellers," I announced in my classes in the fall. "I'd like to invite some folks who really struggle with spelling to work with me on trying to figure out why you struggle and what we can do about it."

We sensed they had much to teach us about ways to support their growth in spelling. We invited these students to work collaboratively with us to develop case studies that would explore their spelling histories, current levels of competence, and overall literacy engagement. By involving the students themselves in this search and by looking both ways—through the lens of what research had to offer as well as through the lens of what our challenged spellers could tell us—we hoped to find ways to support them as spellers and writers.

The middle school, high school, and college students who joined our search all attended public schools, took regular English classes, and came from English-speaking homes. Most came from middle-class families, though some came from slightly upper or lower socioeconomic circumstances. Their school settings ranged from rural areas to small cities that border a major metropolis. In almost every case, our student collaborators had attended schools in the United States for their entire school careers. We made a deliberate choice to focus on this population, knowing that students with bilingual or special education needs would introduce specialized concerns beyond the scope of our inquiry.

To begin, we asked the students in our classes to write personal spelling histories. Generally, spelling histories were handwritten. Because we began our work early in the semester, we chose to gather spelling histories from all students. These papers helped us identify students who may have been struggling with spelling and gave us a first paper to analyze closely. We thought it would be interesting to look at the differences in spelling backgrounds and overall writing skills. Later, we constructed interviews with each of the initial twenty-four student collaborators. The interviews were intended to probe into areas introduced by the students in their written histories.

Analyzing Students' Written Spelling Histories

In the written spelling histories, students were asked to think about how they learned to spell, including support both in and out of school. We wanted to know about the kinds of lingering recollections they might have had that could provide us with clues about their current abilities, attitudes, and concerns. The papers they generated served three broad purposes. First, as an unpolished sample of writing, each paper gave us a glimpse at the individual's unassisted writing abilities and helped us identify spelling strengths and weaknesses. Second, the papers provided a platform from which to begin sifting information about students' spelling journeys to help us think about lessons to support their growth as well as questions to ask during our follow-up interviews. Finally, the spelling histories were intended to help students begin to think about their spelling in a reflective way. We believed the more they reflected upon their spelling, the more aware they would become of their literacy habits. In developing a higher level of reflection, they would also be able to think more strategically about their spelling.

Dawn shared the assignment sheet shown in Figure 2–1 with her students, which she decided to treat as an extra-credit assignment.

I am working with a group of teachers on a research project about the spelling of adolescents. We are looking at many different aspects of how adolescents spell, how they learn to spell, and how they can improve their spelling. You can help us and earn extra credit!

Please write a ROUGH DRAFT (no polishing allowed on this one). It must be HANDWRITTEN (sorry, using a computer would defeat the purpose of this!).

In this draft, please write all you can tell us about

- your early memories of spelling
- spelling in school
- other people's attitudes about spelling (teachers, parents, peers)
- your attitudes about spelling

Figure 2–1. Dawn's Spelling History Assignment

Spelling has been a part of your school experience for a long time. I'm interested in exploring with you what you remember about learning to spell.
How did you learn to spell words at school? What kinds of things did your
teachers do to help teach you to spell? Did you learn words at home? If so,
who helped you and what did they do? How do your parents feel about
spelling? How do you feel about your spelling now?

Use any tools you are accustomed to using. After you turn your papers
in, I'll be looking at them to see what we can learn about the types of mistakes we make and the kinds of support you might need this year.

Figure 2–2. Jennifer's Spelling History Assignment

Though most of us collected rough draft samples like Dawn, Jennifer was
interested in seeing how her students fared at spelling when they used all the tools
they had available. She gave the instructions shown in Figure 2–2 (see Appendix
A for a reproducible spelling history assignment).

We analyzed the spelling histories of our challenged spellers in a variety of
ways. First, we read and noted significant issues discussed by the students. These
included a range of comments, such as the types of spelling instruction the
students remembered, personal beliefs about spelling, and reactions to particular
features of spelling instruction. These comments were carefully logged for future
discussion. Second, we analyzed the writing to determine the total number of
words students used, the number of words they misspelled, and the types of error
patterns these misspellings represented. By doing this, we hoped to gauge the
extent of their spelling difficulties in relation to their overall writing skills and to
more clearly identify the types of errors most prevalent in their work. Jon's and
Kelly's papers (Figures 2–3 and 2–4) are transcribed from handwritten papers. The
errors are italicized for emphasis.

As we read, we find that Jon's problems with spelling date to his early years in
school. Despite parental encouragement, Jon hated spelling and continues to hate
it as a high school student. We learn that spelling tests and his constant sense of
failure with them contribute to his present disdain. Though Jon doesn't tell us
much about the strategies used to teach spelling in school, he does let us know
that spelling was stressed, that he practiced at home, and that words just wouldn't
stay in his head, despite his rehearsal of them in and outside of school.

We learn that he studied "*ruels* and silent letters" and that the experience left
him confused and frustrated. We also find out that Jon recognizes the importance of
spelling beyond school, in "the outside world." He sees himself heading to college

I never *like* spelling as a kid *infact* I still hate spelling. I *rember* that when we had spelling tests in *elementry* school I would fail about all of them. My parents *aloys encurged* me to learn how to spell better but I hated it so much I *diden't* care. I *now* that spelling is a *verey* important part of the outside world and my spelling is getting better but for *sone* reason I never got it. I would go home and *practis* the words and they just *wouldent stoy* in my head I think that all the *ruels* and silent letters confused me more than they did good so I kind of made up my own way of spelling. I just sound out the words and put down the letters and *for get* about dropping letters and all the silent letters. The words that I *new* I could spell with the silent letters but that was it. When I got into middle school my spelling *realey* went downhill because we were learning many more rules about spelling and for a while I *realie diden't* care. Another weird thing is that *sone tines* I will spell a word right and the next time I *right* it I will spell it *diffrent*. I could never figure out why I did that. But now that I am in high school my spelling is *realie* took a turn for the better and I hope that it continues to improve. But I *realer* feel that *befor* I go to *colluge* I *won't* to have my spelling almost perfect because I *now* that in *colloge* the *professers* don't like to see *oney* misspelled words none of the teachers do.

Figure 2–3. Spelling History: Jon (High School)

after high school, and he notes that he hopes to have his spelling improve because he realizes college professors will expect that.

We find out other things from Jon's paper as well. For one, he has mastered some of the conventions of spelling. Of the 285 words Jon has used in his paper, 32 are misspelled, approximately 11 percent of the total words used. Further, he recognizes that he is inconsistent with his spelling, sometimes spelling a word correctly and incorrectly in the same paper. He relies on sounding words out as a primary strategy, and, despite his insistence that he forgets about "dropping letters and all the silent letters," he does know to double the final consonant in a single-syllable word before adding the suffix *-ing*. Moreover, we can see that Jon has both voice and the ability to say what he means in print.

Kelly, a middle school student, provides us with different insights through her spelling history (see Figure 2–4). Kelly uses a total of 293 words in her spelling history, including 28 misspellings. We learn a great deal about Kelly as a student and a writer in this piece. Like Jon, we find her spelling memories range from vague to negative. She is convinced spelling was taught but is unable to recollect how teachers approached instruction. There were tests, which indicates some sort of spelling

My memories of spelling are is that we had spelling *test* every week. I *dont* think that I *like* it very much because it was annoying because you had to study and it is really hard because I am not a good speller. I *probuly* started to write about *forth* grade I am not *sher*. My 6th grade teacher. Some positive things about spelling tests we used to have they helped me to spell better. The bad thing that spelling would be that it was hard for because I had to study and everyone did not really *half* to because it came easy to them.

I *dont no*. I don't *realy* remember how *are* teacher *tote* me spelling. Yes we did have spelling tests. They *where negagative* for me because I would *allways* get bad on them. I think they would give me the words and then you would study them and then they would read them off and you would write them down. I *dont no*.

I *dont* think that I am the best speller but I am OK. I think that my attitude has made me an OK writer. If I can do that *than* I can do anything *thats* how writing has *influeced* me like in school. I go to *shool*. Sometimes I have hard time spelling words. I *dont useally* use a *distionary*, Sometimes I worry about my spelling because I am not very good. The words I *dont no* how to spell big words. They are *to* confusing to *remebe* all of them.

They [her parents] want me to do good in spelling. They annoy me about it all the time. Sometimes, they help me with reading over my papers and stuff. It helps me I guess.

Figure 2–4. Spelling History: Kelly (Middle School)

lists were given. The tests led her to conclude that most other people don't struggle with spelling, but that she does because she finds it so hard. Kelly has internalized the traditional sequence of spelling instruction well. The teacher gave words; she studied them; and then the teacher read them in a test setting while she wrote them down. Noticeably absent from her recollection is any reference to strategies for learning the words or opportunities to use the words in authentic contexts.

Kelly also lets us know that she values writing. In fact, she acknowledges the importance of writing in school and her belief that her attitudes regarding writing are important for her success. Nonetheless, when it comes back to spelling, she admits her lack of strategies. She worries about her poor spelling, admitting her difficulty with big words; yet, she clearly feels spelling is "*to* confusing to *remebe*" and eschews even dictionaries as spelling aids.

Nancy, another middle school student, composed her spelling history on a word processor and had tools like a spell checker available (see Figure 2–5). From

My early memories of spelling, I had a hard time with spelling and I didn't really like it. Well how I learned to spell is I would just spell a word how it sounds. Well I always had a hard time with spelling and I would spell the word and get it wrong all the time. Well I would never do that well because I didn't know how to spell. Well my attitude I hate it because I don't know how to spell that well. I think that is important because spelling counts on your papers. You can't get a good job and *proboly* not *grauate* from high school. I feel *dum* because when people read my paper they have to ask me what the word is. Yes because if you don't know how to spell you are not going to get a good job. Well people think that it is good to know because you have to know how to spell if you want to get a good job. Well they *incorige* me to spell by not telling me how to spell the word. Well they want to help and I think I could do *beter*. Well really I don't know how they *fill* about it.

Figure 2–5. Spelling History: Nancy (Middle School)

her paper we find she's had difficulty with spelling for a long time. By spelling words the way she thinks they sound, she reveals a faulty sense of sound-letter relationships that has resulted in getting words "wrong all the time." Because Nancy feels unsuccessful with spelling, she hates it. Yet, despite her negative feelings about spelling, Nancy apparently places value on it and recognizes that others do as well.

Not only is Nancy, at age thirteen, aware of the importance that teachers place on spelling in written work, but she is already pondering the dismal prospect of not being able to get a good job as an adult because of her poor spelling. Worse still, she has come to think of herself as "*dum* because when people read [her] paper they have to ask [her] what the word is."

Nancy's paper exhibits some distinctive features. She tends to string sentences together and frequently omits or adds words. Errors such as these could be corrected, for the most part, by practicing a strategy of reading her work aloud to herself and listening to how the sentences sound. Her overreliance on *well* as an introductory word detracts from the overall sound and quality of the piece. For most writing teachers, addressing these issues would be first-order interventions because making those corrections would raise the perceived quality of the paper considerably. Nancy's paper contains only 207 words. Of these, only 6 are misspelled. For Nancy, it is not the number of errors that raises the greatest concern, it is the range of errors and the air of hopelessness she projects.

Categories of Errors

As we looked more closely at the misspellings, Mina Shaughnessey's (1977) work with error analysis gave us a platform for discussing the error patterns emerging from these papers. In her work with basic writers, Shaughnessey noted the difficulties her students demonstrated with letter representations that were highly unpredictable: long vowels and such phonemes as *sh*, *er*, *f*, *j*, and the *schwa* sound—the vowel sound that is unstressed in a multisyllabic word—with its twenty-two variant spellings (167). She further noted that these students had not generally seen words enough as readers nor used them enough as writers to make correct choices in spelling. Shaughnessey pointed out that students seldom misspell words randomly; instead, they tend to make particular kinds of mistakes that reflect their background knowledge about spelling and level of spelling development, an observation verified by Reed (1971) and Henderson (in Henderson and Beers 1980).

Shaughnessy created categories of errors to aid in understanding the spelling needs of her students. The categories she created included misspellings caused by unpredictability of the language (described above), misspellings caused by pronunciation, misspellings caused by unfamiliarity with the structure of words, misspellings caused by failure to remember or see words, and homophones (164–174). Misspellings caused by pronunciation account for widely varying errors, reflecting tendencies to drop or add sounds at the ends of words, misrepresenting sounds that may not be heard in speech but are apparent in print (like the sounds *m-n*, *d-t*, *f-v*, and *b-d*), and prefixes that are often difficult to distinguish in spoken English. Structural errors reflect the student's difficulties discriminating among syllables or applying rules for modifying words with prefixes and suffixes.

We chose to develop categories to describe the spelling errors our students made to help us think about the numbers and types of errors in their first and final draft writing. Specifically, we wanted to identify those errors that were most common and those errors that could be addressed most easily. We identified five categories of errors: homophones, errors caused by faulty grammatical knowledge, prefix/suffix errors, errors resulting from incorrect splitting or joining of words, and a broad category of errors that included structural and pronunciation concerns.

We created error analysis charts to use with all first—and later final—draft papers. For example, Jon's chart (Figure 2–6) helped us see that his errors (see Figure 2–3) fell primarily into four categories: homophones/wrong words; structural and pronunciation concerns; faulty grammatical knowledge; and incorrect splitting or joining of words.

Words are sometimes misspelled as a result of faulty knowledge of grammatical concepts. Words like *didn't* and *wouldent* suggest a need to revisit the logic operating in the creation of contractions. Other misspellings, like *rember*, appear

Homophones/wrong words	Structural and pronunciation errors
now (know)	*rember* (remember)
new (knew)	*elementry* (elementary)
right (write)	*aloy* (always)
won't (want)	*verey* (very)
	sone (some)
	stoy (stay)
	sone (some)
	tines (times)
Grammar-related errors	*oney* (any)
like (liked—past tense)	*encurged* (encouraged)
diden't (didn't—contraction)	*realie* (really)
diden't (didn't—contraction)	*practis* (practice)
wouldent (wouldn't—contraction)	*colluge* (college)
	ruels (rules)
	colloge (college)
Errors in splitting or joining words	*realey* (really)
infact (in fact)	*realie* (really)
for get (forget)	*realer* (really)
	befor (before)
	diffrent (different)
	professers (professors)

Figure 2–6. Jon's Error Analysis Chart

to result from faulty pronunciation. Homophones—like *new* for *knew*, *now* for *know*, and *right* for *write*—often prove troublesome for challenged spellers. Spelling errors may also result from inadequate knowledge of sound-letter relationships, specifically the 52 phonemes (sound units) that correspond to 170 graphemic options we have in English (Hanna et al. 1966). Jon told us that he tries to sound out letters as he attempts to get words down on paper. Our chart suggests that he often guesses at the letters to match sounds.

Jon told us that he found the vast array of rules and patterns in English overwhelming. In many cases, his writing suggests that he, perhaps, makes up sound-letter correspondences as he goes along, for example words like *sone* for *some*, *tines* for *times*, and *oney* for *any*. Finally, Jon's lack of knowledge about the structure of words may have resulted in words like *colluge* and *colloge* for *college*. Jon's spelling suggests confusion about how to break words into syllables, substituting incorrect syllables in the middle of words, as well as faulty knowledge of the rules that govern suffixes and prefixes.

The error analysis generated from Kelly's spelling history (shown in Figure 2–7) reveals slightly different areas of concern. When we look at the types of errors Kelly makes in her writing (see Figure 2–4), it's easy to see that two of the most problematic categories really aren't spelling errors at all. Like many other challenged spellers, she finds homophones troublesome.

Kelly uses the word *no* to represent *know* three different times. Learning one homophone would help her correct repeated errors. Similarly, it's clear that she has difficulty with contractions. The word *don't* is consistently misspelled throughout her paper as *dont*. A quick, focused lesson on contractions could likely help her clean up these errors. More complicated are her structural and pronunciation concerns. While in primary school, adept spellers generally learn various within-word patterns governing vowel use in single-syllable words. Through reading and writing, they practice using chunks of language to produce vowel and consonant clusters, gain understanding of the logic that governs doubling or dropping of letters,

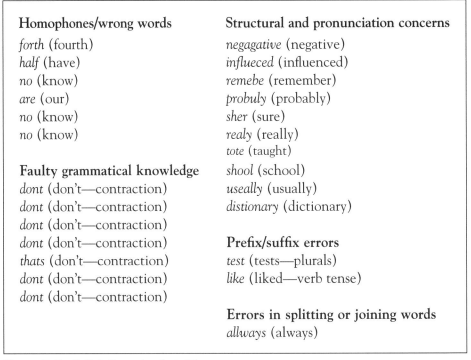

Homophones/wrong words	Structural and pronunciation concerns
forth (fourth)	*negagative* (negative)
half (have)	*influeced* (influenced)
no (know)	*remebe* (remember)
are (our)	*probuly* (probably)
no (know)	*sher* (sure)
no (know)	*realy* (really)
	tote (taught)
Faulty grammatical knowledge	*shool* (school)
dont (don't—contraction)	*useally* (usually)
dont (don't—contraction)	*distionary* (dictionary)
dont (don't—contraction)	
dont (don't—contraction)	**Prefix/suffix errors**
thats (don't—contraction)	*test* (tests—plurals)
dont (don't—contraction)	*like* (liked—verb tense)
dont (don't—contraction)	
	Errors in splitting or joining words
	allways (always)

Figure 2–7. Kelly's Error Analysis Chart

Homophones/wrong words	Structural and pronunciation concerns
fill (feel)	*grauate* (graduate)
	probuly (probably)
	dum (dumb)
	incorige (encourage)
	beter (better)
Faulty grammatical knowledge	
Incorrect splitting or joining words	

Figure 2–8. Nancy's Error Analysis Chart

and acquire knowledge of prefixes and suffixes. Like Jon, Kelly has failed to absorb some of this important information along the way.

Finally, we come to Nancy's writing (see Figure 2–5). Her error analysis chart (see Figure 2–8), reveals difficulties that extend beyond spelling. Nancy has many concerns that are writing-based. These tend to make her spelling errors seem more overwhelming than they are. Of the spelling errors she has made, most reflect phonetic patterns that seem to have been incorrectly or poorly learned.

In all cases, the error analysis charts helped us understand the types and scope of errors most prevalent in our students' writing. Finally, they helped us focus more sharply on the types of support our students would need to address their spelling concerns.

3

Learning from Student Interviews

Looking closely at student writing helped us identify more clearly the types and scope of errors our students tend to make. It also raised many new questions that we needed to answer as we continued to think about providing instructional support for challenged spellers. What more could we learn about the types of instruction, instructional environments, and supports they had experienced as young learners? Would we find a link between early experiences with spelling and students' attitudes, behaviors, and engagement with literacy now?

Planning the Interviews

We invited our students to join us for interviews that were open-ended (see Figure 3–1) and intended to "map the territory" of their spelling backgrounds (Spradley 1979). Though interviews were taped for later review, each session was conducted in privacy and students were assured anonymity. Each interview took approximately an hour. Predictably, these interviews illuminated many observations about the background experiences of our challenged spellers and suggested still more issues to explore.

Student Observations About Spelling Instruction

> *Here's the words, here's some worksheets, learn 'em.*
> —Annie, a middle school student

Not unlike Jennifer's experience or mine, the challenged spellers in our study described remarkably similar early spelling experiences. Though secondary students

- Describe your early memories of learning to spell. Particularly, what types of things helped or hurt your ability to learn to spell?
- How do you describe yourself as a speller—then and now? As a reader? As a writer?
- If someone asks you to spell a word, what happens in your brain? In other words, what processes make it possible for you to spell the word?
- How does your spelling influence your writing and your attitudes about writing?
- When you find yourself trying to write a word you aren't sure of, what strategies do you most often use to spell it correctly?
- What types of words or parts of words tend to give you the most difficulty?
- If you were advising a younger person about how to become an expert speller, what would you tell her?
- What could teachers do now to support you with spelling?

©2003 by Rebecca Bowers Sipe from *They Still Can't Spell?* Portsmouth, NH: Heinemann.

Figure 3–1. Interview Questions

represented four different school districts and college students many more, the practices used to teach spelling fell within patterns that were traditional in many ways, including the use of published spelling programs and weekly lists, exercises, and tests. Interestingly, students suggested that teachers didn't really teach spelling: parents did.

> Teachers in school would give us spelling books and they would have different spelling lessons in them and they would give us practice writing out the words. Then we'd have tests on them on Fridays and I'd go home and study them with my mom and the words I'd miss I'd write like five times out and that's basically it. (Jay, a high school student)

Following the initial word lists on Monday, the actual teaching of spelling was left to text-based exercises—often questionable in their instructional value—and parents. Students talked about words being posted on the refrigerator door for the week; of moms, dads, or grandparents spending considerable amounts of time drilling them on words for the Friday test; and about the time spent writing words over and over to commit them to memory.

Despite the collective time and effort devoted to learning spelling in this way, the results were often less than gratifying. Lori, a high school student, told us, "I don't know, I've always had a hard time spelling. I try so hard but I go blank."

Despite lots of effort and hard work, many challenged spellers, like Lori, described an inability to retain words for the test on Friday and even greater difficulty remembering words for application the next week.

So, what did these students learn from weekly lists and tests? Over and over we heard stories about the overwhelming complexity of spelling as students described their beliefs that every single word in the language has to be memorized individually! Many students, like Jon, a high schooler, failed to see any common features in words on their spelling lists. Others, like Jay, also a high school student, recognized the fact that lists had "a common feature like a silent *e*," but often weren't "sure where the lists came from" or "why the words were on the list anyway."

Perhaps Dan, another high school student, best described the confusion for challenged spellers generated by weekly lists. Following up on an earlier comment he had made about a particular list that had taught the use of *-ly* endings, he explained,

> but the whole thing is when you put the *-ly* on a lot of words because they told us to put the *-ly* on words that end in consonants, then when a word that I knew that had a vowel that had *-ly* on it, like *likely*, I didn't know whether I should keep the *e* or drop the *e* or what to do with that. They wouldn't tell us that part, but they'd give us consonants and *-ly*.

For Dan, lists tended to overteach narrowly defined applications of a principle but failed to situate that knowledge in a context large enough to be useful. Dan needed a broader scope of examples that fit the rule, examples that were exceptions to the rule, and time to think about and practice applying the rule. Unfortunately, for challenged spellers, the carefully constructed lists of traditional spelling texts failed to provide knowledge about words that could be applied in a generalized manner.

Jon's, Jay's, and Dan's concerns were echoed by almost all of the students in our study. Erin, a middle school student, reported, "We were really rushed. There were different things to remember every week, so we couldn't really learn to use the rules with other words or in writing." As I reviewed my own spelling history, I, too, recalled the rush of activity involved in finishing the exercises assigned and the confusion about the relationship between exercises such as a word find, a crossword puzzle, and a series of fill-in-the-blank sentences and learning the spelling and application of words.

For many students, the lack of context and authentic use of words appeared to be counterproductive to learning. While Jon didn't notice any common features in his weekly spelling lists until he was in middle school, Nancy, a middle school student, observed, "[I think] the lists had some common things but each week there was a different one, so there was never any time to do much more than memorize the list. And after a while, they all sort of ran together." The result? Half-learned and inaccessible information that has convinced the students that English spelling is far too complicated for them to figure out.

Weekly spelling tests opened up other areas of concern for challenged spellers as well. Through both interviews and written spelling histories, students told of the emotional toll paid each week as, once again, they were reminded that they were less successful (with spelling, though these feelings generalized across disciplines) than their peers. Though Dan, a high school student, had lots of support from his grandmother, who drilled him all week on the words, he remembered the emotional aspect of spelling most vividly. Relating how his grandmother drilled him weekly, he said,

> that really got me ready for the test, but when it came to the test I'd get nervous or I'd forget something or the rule would slip out of my mind. I was so nervous. I would push my pen down like burning holes through the paper.

Annie, a middle school student, also helped us see the depth of the anguish experienced by many students who struggle with spelling. She wrote,

> I *didn't* like spelling in school. My teachers taught it by giving tests. It was a very *studied* experience for me. I hate them. I studied by reading them and then having some sort of spelling bee against my stepdad. I learn best by spelling out loud with *some one* . . . The worst was 4th grade. I had to have a spelling test every Friday. It had 20 words and 2 really hard big words. I *usally* did bad. I would study and *foget*. Then every word you missed you had to write out 5 times unless you got 5 or more words wrong then you had to write it 10 times.

Even for students who did well on weekly tests, the long-term gains appear questionable. As Mike, a middle school student, reported in his spelling history, "I did okay on the tests and words I got right I could remember for a week or so. Then new words kind of pushed the old ones out and I couldn't remember them any more."

The Strategies They Draw Upon

Effective spellers rely upon multiple strategies—both internally and externally based—in order to spell words correctly. To make our teaching more strategic, we felt it important to survey the full repertoire of strategies that our challenged spellers draw upon and to use this information as a platform for introducing additional strategies. We asked students to discuss what they do when they come to a word they want to write but do not know how to spell. What we came to realize is that some students have developed a rich array of strategies to support their spelling, despite other interferences such as visual memory problems, while other spellers have few strategies to draw upon. However, though some challenged spellers draw upon internally based resources for spelling, the vast majority rely heavily on external support.

Internally Based Strategies

> *In cheerleading we do little chants and stuff like that. I can't spell* rebound *without, like, going through it in my head.*
>
> —Mandy, a high school student

Internally based strategies place the responsibility for spelling correctness with the writer and include strategies like creating associations with other words, using mnemonic devices, putting words to rhythm, creating jingles or songs, and—one of the most unique—tracing words in the palm of one hand with the index finger of the other to remember the feel of the word (see Figure 3–2). Externally based strategies situate responsibility for spelling beyond the writer, often drawing upon editors or other resources. While both internally and externally based strategies are good tools, knowledge and use of both seem vital to independent self-correction.

Adolescent challenged spellers demonstrate a high reliance on sounding words out. For Amanda, the mnemonic chant proved successful as she bridged from sounding words out to using sound as a tool for remembering correct spelling. Putting words to rhythm helped her attempt to spell words she wanted to use in her writing. For Jon, a high school student, use of phonics skills finally began to bridge into use of visual cues. He wrote, "I sound the word out and get as close as I can. Then, I re-arrange letters till it looks right." Students who exhibited internalized strategies reported using strategies like have-a-go, in which a word is written in multiple variations to allow the writer to choose the most correct-looking spelling, and word substitution, in which a word is replaced with another of similar meaning, even if the word is not the best one to use.

- sounding words out
- putting words to rhythms
- have-a-go
- word substitution
- looking for words spelled similarly
- looking for words with the same parts
- mnemonics
- chunking words into syllables
- using root words, prefixes, and suffixes
- using spelling rules
- memorizing words
- applying meaning-based strategies

Figure 3–2. Internally Based Strategies

Other strategies that are less frequently used include mnemonics, word chunking (syllables), rules, and root words. Chunking words into meaning or sound units helps some students gain success by converting words into manageable bits. Interestingly, using mnemonic devices seemed to work for challenged spellers only when they were personalized. For example, Erin, a middle school student, described the usefulness of mnemonics but qualified her endorsement with "but they have to be my own," while other students, like Annie and Ringo, also in middle school, warned that mnemonics can be confusing and counterproductive, a clear indication for us that successful spelling strategies must be individually meaningful for challenged spellers.

Though mentioned by less than 10 percent of the students—and mostly by students at the high school and college levels—rules and meaning-based strategies appear potentially effective for challenged spellers. Unfortunately, even for the students who cited the use of these tools, such strategies appear haphazardly applied, as is illustrated by Mandy, a high school student, who wrote: "I remember the rules, I just don't use them myself . . . usually when I'm trying to spell something, I don't remember them or don't think of them." We identified a strong need for our students to have opportunities to revisit meaning-based spelling cues.

Externally Based Strategies

With challenged spellers, we found a particularly heavy reliance on external strategies, those that place the responsibility for correction outside of the student (see Figure 3–3). These students place the responsibility for correct spelling somewhere beyond themselves—asking Mom or another editor or relying on spell checkers. Their motivation for doing so ranges from fear of embarrassment about their poor spelling to a sense of helplessness about ever being able to manage spelling independently. For example, Joel, a college student, reported, "I have my wife read all my work. I'm constantly worried that my work will look ridiculous or that people will think I don't really care because of my spelling." Joel constantly fears embarrassment about spelling despite his expertise as a writer. Lori, a high school student, on the other hand, appears simply baffled by spelling and eagerly relinquishes responsibility for spelling to more capable hands: "I *apreciate* when she [her mother] helps me because I have no *patients*, but I like when my mom makes it fun, like songs, or games." Lori is willing to use the strategies her mom gives her but consistently cites her own need for outside support.

- asking someone
- using computer spell checkers
- keeping lists
- using a dictionary

Figure 3–3. External Spelling Strategies

Though some use of external resources is, of course, very positive, we were struck by the narrow scope of strategies available to students who overrely on external resources. If there is no one to ask and no spell checker available, the clear tendency is to simply give up. One of the most important things challenged spellers can be taught is how to recognize problems with their own work and seek solutions independently. Placing the responsibility for spelling totally outside themselves puts these challenged spellers in a position of weakness. In these cases, students tend to see spelling as beyond their control. Frequently, they cited other family members who were poor spellers as an explanation for their own weaknesses. Investment in literacy-related activities and a sense of power over literacy clearly affect the willingness of some challenged spellers to seek strategies to address their spelling concerns.

4

Delving Deeper

From the time I was little I thought the spelling of certain words was weird. I would even make jokes about it . . . Let's take the word tomb *for example.* Tomb *is* tomb, *but* comb *is* comb; home *is* home, *but* some *is* some. Some *is* some, *but* numb *is* numb! How can words that sound the same be spelled so differently? Words like* elephant *always made me mad because they had different spellings than their sounds. Where is the* f *in* elephant *or the* a *in* beret, *which should have two as, ba-ray. Not one!*

—Ringo, a middle school student

Our challenged spellers continued to reveal new questions to us. What more could we learn from studying the types of words they could spell and the words that gave them most difficulty? What role did visual memory play in their lack of spelling success? What strategies did they have to draw upon when attempting to spell a word? When given all the tools they needed, what level of self-correction did they demonstrate? Each question led to further collaborative exploration . . . and more questions!

The Words They Know

We chose two approaches to investigate the types of errors our challenged spellers tended to make: a spelling inventory and word analyses comparing first and polished draft writing. While we shared reservations about testing words outside a meaningful context, the list-based tests helped us look for the types of cueing systems students used and offered information that helped us understand the gaps in their spelling development.

Placement Inventories

The placement inventories we used provide a series of lists, with twenty words each, leveled for grades 1 through 8 (Gentry 1997, 44). The student's approximate grade level in spelling is indicated at the point where the student misses half the words on a given list. At that point, the testing stops. For our purposes, we were less concerned about grade-level placement than about the characteristics of the words students were able to spell successfully or unsuccessfully. Because we were able to administer the placement inventories one-on-one, we were able to capture comments made by students, note levels of frustration, and observe strategies they attempted to employ. In actual classroom application, as will be described later, inventories are introduced to whole classes and placed in context so that students will understand their purpose.

Roughly two-thirds of the students in our study group placed at the fifth- or sixth-grade level on the spelling inventory, with the remaining one-third at the seventh-grade level. This included challenged spellers who were returning to school for teacher certification, having already completed undergraduate degrees and, in several cases, successful careers in other fields. Word lists at the fifth- and sixth-grade level included the following types of words:

- possessives and plurals (*women's*, changing *-y* to *- i* to add *-es*)
- silent *-e*, *-ei*, and *-ie* words
- words with prefixes like *bi-*, *tri-*, *mid-*, *il- im-*, and *ir-*
- words with suffixes like *-er*, *-or*, *-ist*, *-ant*, *-am*, *-ist*, and *-ous*
- words with parts like *per-*, *pre-*, *pro-*, *-tion*, and *-cian*
- words from other languages (see Gentry 1997, 36–41)

Looking at our students' performance in light of research by Hughes and Searle (1997) and Gentry (1997) helped us understand more about what created the difficulties our challenged spellers were experiencing. For young learners, the primary cueing system tends to be sound: children spell the way they hear words. Words children learn to read and write in primary school tend to adhere more closely to sound-based cues than words learned later. Growing phonemic awareness learned through reading and writing helps children understand the ways letters or combinations of letters relate to the ways words are spelled.

Whereas most children come to rely on sound, sight, and meaning as strategies for spelling words as they progress, our challenged spellers clung to sounding out words as their primary—and in some cases only—internalized strategy. While others might think about what the word looked like when they saw it written in a book, on the board, or in earlier pieces of writing, our students continued to rely on hearing the sounds of the letters. While others could draw upon rules like *i* before *e* except after *c* and changing *y* to *i* before adding *es* to help them spell words correctly, our students struggled with these strategies, had no knowledge of them, or ignored them altogether. While others could rely on meaning-based strategies like prefixes, suffixes, and roots that help extend student knowledge of the common bases from which words emerge (see Appendix F), our students lacked this crucial information or applied it poorly.

As we looked at the spelling placement scores and student writing and reviewed transcripts of our interviews with our students, we found a heavy reliance on phonics as a primary strategy for spelling. Unfortunately, this strategy can be unreliable, as Annie, a middle school student, described: "I try and sound it out. Usually it looks pretty wrong. I have to write it down and change letters around until it looks right." As long as words were spelled as they sounded, students experienced virtually no problems.

From Rough to Polished Drafts: Abilities to Self-Correct

It is important to reiterate that all the students with whom we worked came from classrooms influenced by writing process philosophies. Students were encouraged to secure responses to their rough draft writing, use computers and other resources to facilitate revision and editing, and approach writing tasks in multiple drafts. Within this environment, we found the range of self-correction behaviors exhibited by students to be astounding.

Excerpts from middle school student Kelly's first and polished drafts, shown in Figures 4–1 and 4–2, demonstrate how some students are able to use spelling resources and the writing process to self-correct many of their spelling errors.

One day in class sitting there *lisining* to the boring teacher I was waiting for the bell to ring so I could go outside and play in the snow and on the ice. It was pretty cold outside so we *where waring scarfs* and big winter coats. "*Ya*" the bell rang everyone jumped up and ran outside. We ran right to the ice where all of *are* friends *where*. We started sliding around we *where* pushing *eachother*. All of a *suden* I fell someone pushed me right on to the ice it was cold I put my hands down but they *sliped* on the ice. Just *liying* there very cold *stuned* that someone pushed me and the pain. I *layed* there on the cold ice I felt on my skin. I did not hear anyone talking everyone just *stod* there in shock. Finally someone helped me up I was *to* weak to stand they had to *carfully cary* me to the teacher, crying *estaralie*. She ran and I *hobeld* down to the office. It felt like it *toke* me a eternity to get there but only about a *coupel* minutes. When we got there they *bandiged* me up and cleaned me off. My *neas where* wet from falling on the ice. I sat in the chair all by myself *wating* while they called my parents to come and get me . . .

Figure 4–1. Kelly's Rough Draft (Transcribed from Handwritten Copy)

"Yea" the bell rang everyone jumped up and ran outside recess time. We ran right to the ice *were* all of *are* friends were. We started sliding around and we *where* pushing each other. All of a sudden I *fell* someone pushed me right on the ice. It was cold. I put my hands down but they slipped on the ice. Just lying there very cold *stunted* that someone pushed me.

The pain it was hard to stand because it hurt so *bad*. I *layed* there on the cold ice. I felt on my skin the wetness of the ice. No one was talking everyone just was silent they *where* in shock. Finally after I've been *laying* there for a while someone picked me up all they asked "are you ok, are you ok. I just said "yes," go get the teacher quick I hardly could stand I was so weak. They had to help me walk over to the teacher I was crying the teacher helped me hobble down to the office.

Once I got there they took me to the room where the bandages and fixed me up. Then they told me the bad news they said you are going to have to get stitches I felt like I was going to faint. They called and told my parents that I was going to *half* to get stitches and come and pick me up immediately. By that time school was almost out. It took them forever to get there.

Figure 4–2. Kelly's Polished Draft (Completed on a Word Processor)

They also help illustrate why spell checkers are insufficient in handling the errors challenged spellers make.

Between the first and polished drafts of Kelly's writing, we see an increase in length from 230 to 250 words and a reduction in the number of spelling errors. In Kelly's class, students participate in a variety of revision activities, ranging from reading the paper aloud to a partner to conferencing with the teacher. We can quickly note the changes in sentence structure; Kelly's polished draft tightens the wording, cleans up many of the sentence errors, and does a better job of placing the reader in the story.

In terms of spelling, there are some obvious differences in the two drafts. In her rough draft, Kelly makes 14 structural and pronunciation errors, 2 errors related to grammatical usage, one suffix error, and one that results from running words together (see Figure 4–3). Upon editing and using a spell checker, Kelly is able to eliminate most of her errors caused by mispronunciations and sound-letter corre-spondence, and errors caused by writing words together. However, homophones remain troublesome for her, as the number of these errors actually increases from five to seven. Homophones are not generally caught by spell checkers, so Kelly

Homophones/wrong words	Structural and pronunciation
Ya (yeah)	**concerns**
are (our)	*lisining* (listening)
where (were)	*estaralie* (hysterically)
where (were)	*waring* (wearing)
to (too)	*suden* (sudden)
	stuned (stunned)
Faulty grammar knowledge	*stod* (stood)
liying (lying)	*carfully* (carefully)
layed (lay)	*cary* (carry)
	hobeld (hobbled)
Prefix/suffix errors	*toke* (took)
scarfs (scarves)	*coupel* (couple)
	bandiged (bandaged)
Incorrect splitting or joining words	*neas* (knees)
eachother (each other)	*wating* (waiting)

Figure 4–3. Error Analysis of Kelly's Rough Draft

clearly needs additional strategies to help her weed homophone errors from her work. For all other errors, it appears critical that she—and other challenged spellers—understand and use all available resources.

Sense of Self as a Reader and a Writer

Several studies raised questions for us about the relationships among reading, writing, and spelling. In one multiyear study of spellers in grades 1–5, active involvement with reading was found to be an indicator of future success with spelling, though the authors reported that "while reading was a necessary condition for good spelling, it was certainly not sufficient" (Hughes and Searle 1997, 124). Other researchers, like Frank Smith, suggest that "fluent reading per se has little facilitative effect upon learning to spell" (Smith, cited in Henderson 1980, 6–7). And, while reading appears to correlate for many students with success in spelling, good spelling may not necessarily depend on strong reading skills. Many of our challenged spellers demonstrated both interest and strength in reading and writing and appeared to be excellent students. Was there a combination of factors that supported some challenged spellers in overall literacy growth that might be missing for others?

Challenged spellers in elementary grades seem marked by a sense of inadequacy and a lack of self-efficacy: "This group of children did not see themselves as having any inner resources to call upon when trying to spell a word other than 'sounding out,'" and "from the beginning . . . poor spellers perceived spelling to be weird and arbitrary" (Hughes and Searle 1997, 80, 81). Certainly some of the challenged spellers in our classes demonstrated the same sense of being awash in the language and were as mystified with spelling and bereft of strategies as the struggling spellers in these studies focused on elementary grades.

As we continued to work with this population, we came to find that our challenged spellers demonstrated tremendous variation in their enthusiasm for and investment in reading and writing. We began to look at student interviews with an eye toward understanding the role of internal locus of control as a factor relating to the ability to self-correct spelling in final drafts and to the ability to keep the role of spelling in perspective—as a part of writing and not as writing itself. In the process, we were struck by the critical importance investment in either reading or writing held for challenged spellers.

Those students who expressed a sense of being in charge of their own literacy were generally able to see spelling as a small part of the writing process and develop strategies for spelling. Students who demonstrated a lack of control over their own reading or writing generally carried that sense of helplessness into their spelling. Student enjoyment of both translated to heightened investment in literacy. When students were invested in literacy—as evidenced by playing with language, writing stories, letters, or journals, or luxuriating in a good book—they were able to compensate for severe difficulties with spelling. When they did not have this investment, spelling tended to seem overwhelming.

The Role of Visual Memory

Because spelling is widely described as a visual skill, we investigated the role visual memory played in the spelling difficulties experienced by our students. More than one-half of our challenged spellers demonstrated substantial difficulty with short-term and/or long-term visual memory, based on Trahan and Larrabee's (1983, 1988) Continuous Visual Memory Test (CVMT), while most others exhibited moderate difficulty. The students who demonstrated substantial visual memory difficulty tended to place at the fifth- or sixth-grade level on the spelling inventories. Because visual cueing systems were less available to challenged spellers, as demonstrated by their difficulty with visual memory, a strong grasp of meaning-based spelling strategies would be even more imperative. Unfortunately, these too appeared to be largely missing from their repertoire of strategies, as noted earlier.

However, despite short- and long-term visual memory difficulties, what was most interesting for us was the inconsistency with which visual memory scores correlated with both the ability to edit for spelling in final draft writing and the levels of frustration students expressed regarding spelling! In fact, some students who demonstrated the most pronounced visual memory problems had created a plethora of strategies to accommodate their weaknesses when given the opportunity to use resources for editing. On the other hand, some students who appeared to have minimal difficulty with visual memory tended to have a sense of overwhelming confusion associated with spelling words correctly.

As we examined our findings about visual memory in light of the spelling histories and stories shared by our students, we were reminded that early spelling instruction relies heavily on visually based strategies. Whether those strategies require writing words over and over, writing words into blanks, searching for words in word finds, writing words in shape boxes, or matching words and definitions, the prevalence of visually based strategies in basal spellers strongly suggests the need to include other strategies that are auditory, kinesthetic, and meaning-based as well.

5

Profiles of Challenged Spellers

Just as researchers describe categories of readers to help understand varying motivations and learning needs (Early 1960; Carlsen 1974; Beers 1998), we began to see categories emerging as we examined the case studies of our challenged spellers. These helped us understand both the differences in these learners and the complex interplay that exists between literacy investment and sense of personal control. We found that, instead of looking at all challenged spellers in the same way, we had to probe deeper if we were to effectively support their growth in our classrooms.

The four categories we identified are shown in Figure 5–1. Though these categories provide descriptive information about different types of challenged spellers, they are by no means intended to be mutually exclusive. Instead, the categories reflect a sliding scale that highlights differences in engagement with literacy, sense of personal control over language and learning, and personal motivation. Examining the profiles of students in each of these categories helps to detail their reasons for poor spelling performance and suggests potential strategies for building spelling strength, promoting language awareness, and developing a sense of competency as language users.

Category One Challenged Spellers

> *I do a bit of writing. When we were kids, we came up with a story line—a Dungeons and Dragons type of thing—just as a joke. I came up with this character and I started making a story behind him, so I started writing that. And, yeah, I'm still writing it, too.*
>
> —Dan, a high school student

Category One: Full Literacy Life	Category Two: Literacy at Arm's Length
<ul><li>exhibits strong reader behaviors; enjoys specific types of books</li><li>exhibits strong writer behaviors; writes for a variety of purposes; writes outside of school</li><li>exhibits a strong sense of personal control over reading and writing; knows own strengths and weaknesses</li><li>uses multiple self-correction strategies, both internally and externally based</li><li>sees spelling as secondary to meaning and as an editing issue</li><li>impact of visual memory unclear</li><li>enjoys language</li><li>actively uses and advocates multiple drafts in writing</li></ul>	<ul><li>exhibits average reader behaviors; can read but often chooses not to</li><li>exhibits average writer behaviors; does school assignments but little personal writing outside of school</li><li>demonstrates little sense of personal control over language</li><li>uses few strategies for spelling; relies mostly on external resources like spell checkers, peers, and parents</li><li>tends to spell known words correctly; has few strategies for spelling unknown words</li><li>exhibits many gaps in knowledge of spelling rules, patterns, and generalizations</li><li>exhibits weak visual memory recall and very weak delayed visual memory recall</li><li>seeks assistance with editing</li></ul>
Category Three: Literacy Resistance	**Category Four: Literacy Avoidance**
<ul><li>exhibits reluctant reader behaviors; reads when told to</li><li>exhibits weak writer behaviors; does not write outside of school</li><li>demonstrates minimal sense of control over language and learning</li><li>uses external spelling strategies like spell checkers, peers, and adult editors</li><li>seeks editing help from external sources</li><li>exhibits little personal ownership for own writing and spelling</li><li>demonstrates minimal motivation to achieve in spelling</li><li>exhibits weak visual memory</li><li>demonstrates overreliance on phonics</li></ul>	<ul><li>exhibits weak reader behaviors; actively dislikes reading</li><li>exhibits weak writer behaviors; does no writing out of school; may not complete school writing</li><li>demonstrates no sense of personal control over language or learning</li><li>uses few spelling strategies: spelling happens or it doesn't</li><li>identifies self as "bad" at spelling; does not appear to have any ideas on how to improve spelling</li><li>views spelling as important only for grades</li><li>demonstrates overreliance on phonics</li><li>equates poor spelling with being poor at writing and at English</li></ul>

Figure 5–1. Descriptive Categories of Challenged Spellers

While some of our challenged spellers expressed great reluctance with reading, others found reading to be both an enjoyable and an important part of daily life. Like Dan, Category One students exhibit a sense of pleasure in literacy activities. Often actively engaged in reading and writing both in and out of school, these students nonetheless struggle with spelling. For them, however, spelling is perceived as an inconvenience, and strategies for dealing with spelling are readily available.

Dan reads prolifically. Though he describes himself as a "really, really slow reader," he believes that he learned to read well because he took the time and "figured out what the words meant." Dan is a very articulate young man who describes his lack of motivation for school reading—" . . . see Spot run . . . not my idea of fun"—and contrasts that with his passion for science fiction. As a young adult reader, he chooses books "just to read," loves science fiction, and reports that the shortest books he's reading now range between 250 and 300 pages.

Dan's interest in language is evident in his writing as well, despite getting off to a labored start. He describes early school writing as "a lot of . . . reports that weren't really fun" and explains that this type of writing "deterred me from reading and everything." Dan uses multiple drafts for all writing that is important, that is, all writing for which he feels ownership and interest.

Dan spends time with friends who write. Sometimes they even write together. He describes one story that has evolved over time, and how, when he finishes with an episode, he prints that one and writes a new one. Dan's writing is usually kept within his circle of friends. He describes one friend as "avid about writing" and says, "he's got three or four stories going at once and he loves to write."

What about spelling? Dan says, "Well actually, most of the time I don't even pay attention to spelling when I'm doing real quick writing. After all, spelling counts mostly in English class, though it's also important when trying to influence someone." Dan is a student who sees himself as capable and in charge of his own literacy. He demonstrates a sense of confidence about writing. Though he missed half the placement test words on the sixth-grade inventory—particularly, dropping letters in words like *arrangement* (*arrangment*), adding letters in words like *theme* (*theame*), spelling many words the way they sound to him, like *burden* (*birden*), and reversing letters in words like *yield* (*yeild*)—and has pronounced difficulty with within-word patterns in his first draft writing, for him, spelling is just a tool he uses in writing to help him communicate with his readers.

Dan uses words in writing deliberately and seldom substitutes an inferior word just because he can't spell a more appropriate one. He describes a series of strategies he uses to get to the correct spelling of a word, from internally based ones to using outside editors. In first draft writing, Dan says he will "just go for it," creating an approximate spelling as a placeholder for future editing. He does this by "chunking [the word] up by sound" and then "trying to see it" in his head. For later drafts, he can look up the word, run a spell check, or check with an editor. For Dan, having the opportunity to revise and edit distinguishes work that's important. Without drafts, spelling is apt to be a hazard to his success. With the opportunity for multiple drafts, it is unlikely that spelling will affect his vision of himself as a writer.

Zeek, a high school student, has always entertained a love/hate relationship with language. As a child, he grew up thinking "our English language was the stupidest language where there's all these silent letters and words like *home* and *come* and those that are spelled the same but they're not." Though Zeek cites numerous strategies he uses now—from use of environmental print with words like *depot* to association with words like *secretary* (*secret-ary*)—he rejected being told to "just sound it out," a strategy that Zeek says "got him in trouble" as he attempted words like coincidence: "I know there's no *w* in there," he writes, "but it sounds like there's one so it's *kinda* messed up on that."

Now, Zeek has difficulty with homophones and words that aren't spelled the way he thinks they sound. For example, in *contradictions* (*counterdictions*) he pronounces, and hence hears, sounds that aren't there. In *realize* (*relies*), he fails to hear part of the word.

Like Dan, Zeek has managed to put spelling in perspective through writing. He describes a fourth-grade teacher who became his "favorite teacher of all time."

> She made us *wright* long extensive stories that usually had a theme. In my stories I was complimented on my ideas and the great plot and suspense, though at the same time I was shown the *arrears* I made in my spelling. All my stories really lacked was spelling, *witch* is an easy thing to fix though time consuming.

As an adolescent writer, Zeek is highly invested in his own literacy. He reads constantly, taking a book to the pool or reading in the car as he travels the two and a half hours between his parents' homes or to his grandparents' house. He says, "any free time I like to sit down with a book." His writing is important to him as well, and he spends time creating pieces that are entertaining: "I like to write and I like to read what I write. I like to write what I read . . . you know, just a nice, funny, well-developed story."

How does spelling affect Zeek's writing? Given the opportunity to revise and edit, he doesn't see spelling as a major problem. He describes a favorite procedure for spelling a word correctly: writing the word several different ways to see which looks the best (have-a-go). Often, he keeps scratch paper close by for that purpose. He doesn't remember being taught a strategy like this; he just invented it on his own. Sometimes he admits to "deliberately avoiding a word because [he doesn't] know how to spell it or doesn't *wanna* look it up." For Zeek, time, multiple drafts, and investment are critical ingredients to creating polished pieces of writing. The only time spelling becomes a major obstacle for him is when these are not present.

Ringo, a middle school student, describes his first draft spelling as "trash" because he's "just trying to get ideas down in that draft." As a reader and as a writer, Ringo radiates confidence. He enjoys science fiction, particularly works by Babe Duncan, and cites both the strength of his voice and his use of details as distinguishing characteristics of his own writing.

Ringo has some difficulty with homophones that results in the use of wrong words spelled correctly. Spelling words the way they sound to him takes Ringo to nonstandard spellings, like *arrears* for *errors*. In one first draft sample, he misspelled 36 percent of the words he used. Upon analysis, however, these words fell into only three categories, with homophones being by far the most dominate concern, making his errors easier to address.

Ringo has numerous strategies that he draws upon for spelling. Like Dan and Zeek, he sounds words out, chunks them into parts, and writes them multiple ways. He insists that he would "never abandon a word [he] couldn't spell because [he] knows once it gets to final draft time, [he'll] figure it out." He tells classmates, "Don't be afraid to take chances with your word. Just because you spelled it wrong doesn't mean it's over."

Zeek, Dan, and Ringo represent students who share a commitment to their own literacy. Compared with other challenged spellers, these three demonstrate minimal difficulty with visual memory. Though each of these students placed at the sixth- or seventh-grade level on the spelling inventory and routinely experiences difficulty with spelling many high-use words, each also identifies multiple ways to address spelling errors in final draft writing.

Category Two Challenged Spellers

> *No, I guess I really don't enjoy it [writing]. I mean, if I have to I'll do it and, you know, I don't mind it . . . but I guess I don't really care for doing it in my spare time.*
>
> —Mike, a middle school student

Category Two describes challenged spellers who keep literacy at arm's length. Though capable of reading and writing, these students tend to avoid these activities, often doing only that which is necessary. Unlike Category One spellers, these students tend to have fewer strategies to draw upon; many of their strategies reflect a shift to greater dependence on external resources.

Mike shies away from reading and writing. He says, "I'm not a big reader, though my mom really wants me to read a lot and she's a big reader herself."

Though he avoids reading books outside of school, he enjoys magazines some-times, particularly hunting magazines and *Sports Illustrated*. For reading to be of value, it must fit his interests. Though Mike and his teacher both agree that he is an excellent writer, when asked if he sees himself *as* a writer, he responds emphatically, "No!" He says he'll complete required writing assignments but won't write on his own.

Mike sees no relationships among his reading, writing, and spelling. He insists that he doesn't learn any new words from his reading, though writing is a differ-ent story. Writing forces him to try out new words. He is willing to try words even if he doesn't have the correct spelling for them.

As a speller, Mike struggles. In his spelling history, he recalls numerous spelling tests, which he hated. His spelling may be hampered by his low visual memory skills. Nonetheless, he has compensated with a number of strategies, one of which is sounding it out. Mike reports, "Usually how I spell is, I'll sound it out. Probably chunk by chunk." When asked how he would spell a longer word, like *accommodate*, he glances up, says the word, and spells "*a-c-c . . . o . . . e-a-t-e*," a strategy he used numerous times when taking the placement inventory. In the process of sounding out and chunking the word, whole parts slip away.

Other strategies that Mike routinely uses are asking the teacher or another editor, using a thesaurus (interestingly, Mike says he never uses a dictionary), sub-stituting a word he already knows, or "just plugging in the word" in a rough draft. Mike reports, "I don't feel that my rough drafts need to be good so I'll just . . . if I have any clue . . . I'll just write it and I won't think about it [until later]." His drafts illustrate this. Often words appear to be placeholders as he rushes along with his story. For example, we find words like *barley* (*barely*), *unforcanly* (*unfor-tunately*), and *desprat* (*desperate*). In addition, Mike uses double letters and adds suffixes in a fairly random manner, opening lots of opportunities for strategic teaching by focusing minilessons on high-use rules and patterns.

In addition to tests, Mike remembers that spelling lessons were structured to teach particular types of skills. Unfortunately, the instruction failed to stick with him: "I guess they taught us some rules. But, I guess I don't really remember any of them." Knowing these rules would be helpful, he acknowledges.

Mike distinguishes between writing that is important to him and writing that just counts. If the writing is important, he values multiple drafts. Once he sees a word in writing often, he can generally tell if it is spelled correctly or not, though he generally cannot recall the correct spelling on his own. If there's a problem, he knows to seek out assistance.

Ron, a high school student, describes background experiences similar to Mike's. His spelling history revealed tests and lists that he "abhorred," penalties of multiple copying of misspelled words, phonics workbooks, and multiple-choice exercises. Ron engaged in traditional, basal-supported spelling lessons from first grade to seventh grade. Unfortunately, Ron didn't learn the rules and patterns being taught well enough to apply them consistently in his writing. For example, he describes one rule he was taught as "you'd add an *ie* instead of a *y* if you have an *s* after . . . ." As his voice trails off, it is apparent the rule provided no usefulness. For him, there was insufficient opportunity to integrate and apply spelling facts, and as a result, much of his instruction was of little lasting value to him as a writer.

Ron does like to read books of his choice and frequently dips into horror or humorous books. He discusses favorite authors by name, including John Saul, and he speaks favorably about his mom buying books for him. He makes a clear distinction between his difficulties with spelling and his reading: "I never really had a problem with reading; it's just like spelling and stuff, I'm not good at it." Ron is capable of writing though he reports that he doesn't really like or enjoy it. For him, writing is very "mood dependent." He must be in "certain moods or something or else [he] can't do it."

Using a computer is also important for Ron. Without the opportunity to produce multiple drafts and use a word processor for revision and editing (particularly spell checking), he would "have a lot of stuff wrong." In addition to homophone errors and use of wrong words, Ron appears to have learned incorrect letter representations for some sounds. Words like *sielent* and *simpliest* are examples. In addition, Ron's writing reflects an array of troubles, such as not punctuating contractions correctly, blending words like *alittle* and *alright*, and not remembering to double letters in words like *annoying*.

Ron has other strategies that he uses as well. In addition to sounding out words and chunking them in syllables, he sometimes types the chunks and lets his computer find matches through the spell checker. Often this helps him find the correct spelling. He also uses a dictionary sometimes or searches for another word that "sounds like it and modif[ies] it a little." When Ron wants to write, spelling does not prevent him from doing so.

Josh, a capable high school reader and writer who shares many characteristics with Mike and Ron, chooses to do neither unless he feels highly motivated to do so. Josh reads technical materials, nonfiction informational texts, and newspapers. Like Mike, he cites *Sports Illustrated* as his favorite magazine. Novels are never a first choice for reading material. Though he has written scripts, newspaper articles, and an array of required pieces for school, he writes very little outside of school—and nothing without a keyboard if at all possible. First draft writing is filled with spelling errors that are generally cleaned up in the revision process.

Josh has a number of strategies that he uses to work toward correct spelling in final drafts. He is highly sound dependent. Sounding out and chunking words help him arrive at acceptable placeholders. The use of a spell checker is essential for him (he relied on devices like Franklin spellers in earlier grades). Over the past few years, he has worked with his mom to learn rules and generalizations that he now uses with a degree of accuracy. First draft writing on a computer provides a tremendous sense of freedom, as it allows him to concentrate on the generation of meaning instead of the construction of words. Because he uses a word processor, multiple drafts have become more practical and, hence, the quality of his writing—including voice, organization, and word choice—has improved.

Josh's first draft spelling is very phonetic. Often, he spells words the way they sound to him. For example, we find words like *weal* (*wheel*), *expretion* (*expression*), and *mistereis* (*mysterious*). In middle school, he averaged two or more spelling errors per sentence. As a high school student he has more strategies to draw upon, which has raised both his confidence about writing and his competence with spelling.

Mike, Ron, and Josh represent students who demonstrate a level of ownership for their spelling. Unfortunately, their reluctance to engage in reading and/or writing independently tends to hamper their overall investment in literacy. As spellers, these students have fewer strategies to draw upon than do Category One spellers. The strategies they do have tend to reflect a sense of personal responsibility and ownership, though they are clearly more willing to allow others to take charge of editing tasks than are Category One spellers.

Category Three Challenged Spellers

> *I think we went* through *it, but I don't remember any of it. I don't remember any information from what* they *did. [emphasis added]*
> —Annie, a middle school student

Category Three spellers move from avoidance to resistance in regard to engagement with reading and writing. Students representing this category complete reading and writing tasks when told to but seldom engage in them on their own. These students demonstrate little sense of personal control or ownership for their own reading and writing. Their strategies are limited and generally externally based. Moreover, one finds little motivation in them to achieve in spelling or writing.

Annie, a middle school student, recalls weekly tests, lists, and writing words five or ten times each as the core of her early spelling instruction. What she doesn't recall are any common features represented by the spelling lists nor any instruction in rules, patterns, or generalizations that would support the spelling of new words. Two observations emerge from Annie's statement that opened this section. First, for Annie, spelling was something she went *through*, as one might go through a ceremony or event; second, her reference to what *they* did provides a glimpse into her understanding that instruction—and possibly learning—is passive and other-oriented. Annie sees herself as a poor speller who can "do . . . like . . . little words." However, when it comes to "the big words," she says, "I can't really spell them." Even in her own writing, she has difficulty distinguishing correctly spelled words from ones that are incorrect.

Annie approaches both reading and writing with great reluctance. Interestingly, she recalls enjoying reading as a younger student. Somewhere around fifth or sixth grade, she found herself dreading reading time, frustrated because she couldn't remember "all the stuff [she] was reading unless [she] read it over and over again." She reports that she "used to read every night" but that she doesn't "do it anymore." Describing herself now, she says, "I hate reading. I never read." Still, a few magazines hold her interest, but no books. She describes her writing as very dependent on her mood and interest. Instead of viewing written communication as growing through multiple drafts, she says an acceptable paper materializes if she has interest. Strategies for arriving at clear prose are not readily available to her.

Annie describes her dominant strategy for spelling as "ask somebody." She relies on external support because she can't visualize the word and has no other strategies upon which to draw. When asked what she does to recall the word the next time she needs it, she notes that she will probably have to ask someone again because it's hard for her to remember all the words she needs to know. She has lots of difficulty with silent letters and words that are spelled differently than they sound. She frequently substitutes words she knows for words she doesn't, though sometimes she can't really tell when words are incorrect.

Annie missed half of the words on the fourth-grade placement test. In her writing some words are misspelled in ways that are easy to explain: homophones, like *to/too* and *whole/hole*; incorrectly formed contractions like *Im* (*I'm*); and incorrect application of suffixes, like *happend* (*happened*) and *stoped* (*stopped*). In addition to these errors, others are more difficult to address: words like *sleept* (*slept*), *repetivly* (*repetitively*), and *rember* (*remember*). With *sleept*, it is likely that Annie is overgeneralizing from the present tense of *sleep*, adding a suffix that is sound-based and not rule-based. Both *repetivly* and *rember* are examples of dropping syllables or letters as she pronounces the words. Annie's severe visual memory limitations are likely a complicating factor.

When her work will be graded, Annie takes advantage of peer editors and wants her teachers to correct her spelling in rough drafts. Interestingly, she observes that her spelling was probably better when she read and wrote more. Instinctively, she sees a tie between exposure to language and an ability to figure out spelling. Still, she lacks a sense of being able to address her own problems.

Kelly, another middle school student, recalls spelling lessons and tests through sixth grade. However, she insists that she wasn't taught rules, like *i* before *e* except after *c*, and she says her parents taught her spelling. Kelly demonstrates moderate difficulty with visual memory and missed almost half of the words on the fifth-grade placement list.

Reading and writing are both activities that Kelly resists. She says of reading, "I really kind of don't like to read." For her to read a book, she must "get into the book a lot." Reading dictated by someone else, on the other hand, generally will not be read. In Kelly's words, "if someone tells me to just start it [an assigned book], I would be a little . . . ah, I don't want to . . . ." When asked about recreational reading, Kelly indicates that she would choose to read only if there was nothing else she could do.

Writing is a struggle for Kelly because even when she knows what she wants to say, she has difficulty "getting it down on paper how [she] wants it." She does maintain a journal at home, and she likes that type of writing "'cause it's kind of like [she's] talking to someone else [to] tell them about [her] feelings and stuff." With formal pieces, she relies on process writing because in her first draft she just tries to get things down. She likes to have someone else go over the piece to help her work on sentence structure and spelling. She notes that she always does poorly on writing that is completed in timed situations like tests.

Spelling is a particular problem for Kelly. She tends to freeze up on words she doesn't know. Her dominant strategies are to try to sound out the word and then to ask someone. She describes her frustration when trying to dredge a word from her mind: "I try to picture it in my mind, how I would spell it, but sometimes it's not exactly there—it's like, where did it go?" Occasionally, Kelly has difficulty with words she does know how to spell, particularly if she stops to think about them. Then they, too, disappear. Examples from her error analysis illustrate that she has difficulty with homophones, such as *your* (*you're*) and *to* (*too*). In addition, her analysis demonstrates deeper concerns about spelling: words such as *couper* (*couple*), *panect* (*panicked*), *sher* (*sure*), *hobeld* (*hobbled*), and *toke* (*took*) illustrate a need to revisit the ways in which letters and sounds match. Kelly's lack of spelling control (more than fifty words were misspelled in her spelling history) tends to leave her feeling overwhelmed.

If Kelly has a sense of what she wants to say, she will sound out the word as best she can and then go back. However, sometimes she is not able to decipher the word later. She reports that she "needs time to focus on things and time to focus on words that are going to be important in life." Kelly needs strategies, rules, and generalizations that work with large groups of words.

Jay, a high school student, begins his spelling history by writing about first-grade tests. He describes doing "different activities in the spelling books to memorize how to spell the words." Then he'd go home and study the words with his mom, taking a mock test and writing the words he missed five times. School activities included "matching spelling words and filling in blanks." As the years progressed, Jay experienced "the same kind of books, just different words in each book every year." While he's sure the teachers must have explained the common features of the words, he "doesn't remember that part." He does recall learning spelling rules, but the only one he remembers is "*a before e except after vowels.*" What did he think of spelling instruction? "It was boring." For Jay, it was also ineffective.

As an adolescent, Jay sees himself as "an OK writer" who does "no writing out of school." He insists that he could write if he wanted to; he just doesn't like to write. For example, if he needed to write a letter to a relative, he could. For him, having the chance to do more than one draft is important because he makes numerous errors in his first draft. Jay prefers to work on a computer because it makes editing for spelling easier.

Just as with writing, Jay is able to read but generally chooses not to. He says, "I wasn't much of a big reader, and I'm still not. I can read fine now, but I don't read a lot. I *use* to have trouble in elementary school, and I'd get help with it. I had trouble sounding out words, and I had problems comprehending words, too." Jay prefers magazines about sports or trucks and newspapers to books.

As a speller, Jay is very reliant on spell checkers and editors. His delayed visual memory—the ability to recall words or symbols over time—seems to make it hard for him to remember words, which perhaps partially explains his fifth-/sixth-grade placement on the spelling inventory. He has difficulty with homophones, but within-word structure errors account for most of his spelling concerns: words like *awate* (*await*) and *beileve* (*believe*) are examples.

Mostly, his strategies are externally based, with using electronic spell checkers and asking mom topping the list. As a legal secretary, his mother is an excellent speller. He describes himself and his dad as poor spellers and says of his mom, "[she] takes care of both of us!" Though Jay can visualize words that he knows well, other words he might sound out or try to find in a dictionary if he really wants to use them.

Annie, Kelly, and Jay represent a group of challenged spellers who tend to place responsibility for their spelling on externally oriented sources. Clearly, these students tend to have a diminished sense of personal control over their own reading, writing, and spelling, reflecting less investment in their own literacy than students in Categories One and Two.

Category Four Challenged Spellers

> *I have no* patients . . . *I get a knot in my* stomac *thinking about* school writing . . . Im *so lazy.*
>
> —Lori, a high school student

The difficulties of Category Four challenged spellers go far beyond spelling itself. These students struggle with reading and writing and may actively avoid even school assignments that require either. For this group, language—and sometimes learning—is seen as beyond their individual control. Category Four students possess severely limited strategies for spelling, tend to equate poor spelling with poor writing, and reflect a negative self-esteem.

Middle schooler Dirk's spelling history is noteworthy as much for what he does not remember as for what he does. He remembers lists and tests and contends the words "came from the teacher's book or [she] made them up." The lists seemed to have no unifying features except that the teacher decided words for him to study. Just as many other parents did, Dirk's attempted to help him memorize words at home. He has no recollection of doing anything with spelling in school other than taking tests. Though Dirk missed almost half the words on the fourth-grade placement test, he feels that tests such as the ones he had in elementary school are helpful. Nonetheless, he is unable to articulate why he believes this to be the case.

Dirk experienced difficulty with reading early in school. He describes working with a tutor who helped him learn phonics. When asked what the tutor did in their sessions, he responds, "She did the chunks like *ae, ao,* and stuff like that." Dirk does not see himself as a reader. He'll read things assigned in school if he has to, but he never reads at home. He writes, "I don't like to read If I don't *half* (have) to." Not only does he not like to read, but he finds reading difficult.

Writing is not a strength for Dirk either. Though he describes himself as an "OK writer," he says that his writing "depends on [his] mood." If he feels "into it," he can do the work. Otherwise, he can't seem to accomplish much. Dirk says he doesn't care if his words are spelled wrong in his writing as long as he can figure out what he's saying.

Dirk has many problems with plurals and homophones. Many of his other spelling errors are the result of his excessive reliance on sounding out words. He says he "sounds out tough words in chunks" and he always spells a word aloud to hear the way it sounds. Then he writes the word down as it sounds to see what it looks like. Sadly, Dirk reads very little, so recognizing the correct appearance of words is hardly a viable strategy. As a result, he spells words the way they sound to him with few other cues to assist him in spelling correctly. For example, in one piece of writing he included words like *durby* (*derby*), *prise* (*prize*), and *scupped* (*scooped*). Though he repeats words aloud as an aid to spelling, he tends to drop syllables when doing so. As a result, one finds words like *intered* (*interested*) and *rember* (*remember*) among his frequent errors.

Dirk acknowledges in his written spelling history that his parents feel "spelling is *vary importin* [very important] . . . because spelling is a big part of your grade." However, beyond parental opinions and grades, Dirk seems to have no sense that spelling is important to him personally, to his writing, or to his editing. His investment in reading and writing is tenuous. Dirk appears to have no notion of how to improve his spelling performance. Beyond sounding it out and asking someone, his strategies for correction are, by and large, lacking.

Jon, a high school student, describes his early spelling experiences as "lots of lists and quizzes—just isolated lists of words." It wasn't until middle school that Jon began to recognize patterns in words. At that point, a teacher reintroduced vowel patterns, presumably to help the students revisit some of their spelling generalizations. Now, Jon says he just tries to put letters with sounds, resulting in words like *sceduil* (*schedule*).

Jon is emphatic about his lack of enjoyment of writing. Outside of school, he doesn't write at all—no notes, letters, or journals. Reading has always been problematic for him as well. In school he reads what he has to; outside of school he tends to not read at all. In particular, he identifies long words as more difficult to read.

In terms of strategies for spelling, Jon is limited. He relies heavily on sounding out words. Sometimes he might look up words, though generally he is unable to find them. Most often, he'll ask someone to spell the word for him. He says that he might use peer editors, but he prefers to ask his friend, teacher, or parent. When he uses a spell checker, he seldom rereads to see if the words are correct. Jon says that he feels as though his spelling background has lots of gaps. Because he seems to have no sense of how to address his spelling needs, he suggests, "It's just something I can't do—spell really good—and I accept it."

Lori, another high school student, has few recollections of learning to spell. Though she remembers tests and her mom's efforts to help her, she offers no specifics about spelling—except doing poorly on every test she ever took. In response to every query about learning to spell, she responds, "I don't know . . . I don't remember." Lori does know that she's "bad at spelling." She appears to have no idea why this is so or what to do about it.

Neither reading nor writing is enjoyable for Lori. She resists reading and writing in school and never engages in either for recreation. Lori seems to struggle to find things to write about. She is unable to cite a favorite genre or author. She feels she has always had a hard time with spelling. Despite how hard she tries, she says, "[she] always [goes] blank."

Lori's limited spelling strategies are almost completely externally based. Beyond sounding out words, she describes using spell checkers and her mom. When asked what she does when she comes to a word she can't spell in a paper, she responds, "I'd just spell it the way I can and then I'll circle it and then have my mom check it." Because of her reliance on editors—generally her mother, then a family member, and finally a friend—she prefers to have more than one draft to clean up her spelling. She appears to have no notion of how to improve her spelling performance, and beyond sounding out words and asking someone, her strategies for correction are lacking. Her investment in reading and writing is minimal. She seems to have no sense of control over her literacy life.

For Dirk, Jon, and Lori, far more than spelling is a concern. In each case, a pronounced separation from positive feelings about literacy works against the student. Clearly a problem for each of these students, spelling is a small piece of the overall picture of their literacy engagement. Before spelling takes on real significance, each of these students will need to interact positively with literacy, which will lead, we hope, to a sense of investment in reading, writing, and, eventually, spelling.

Synthesizing Information from the Four Categories

Though lines blur between categories of challenged spellers (see Figure 5–1), a number of traits tend to fall along a continuum. Clearly, issues related to a sense of personal control are significant. In Category One, challenged spellers who are capable of self-correction have thought about their spelling problems and decided to take action. Their numerous strategies range from using spell checkers to setting problematic words to music. Many of these students describe a fascination with language and enjoy playing with words. They appear to be in control of their language, their literacy, and their lives. They acknowledge that spelling is a problem for them and identify ways they will contain the problem. Though often embarrassed about their limitations with spelling, none of these students expressed the notion that spelling would be a major consideration in deciding upon classes to take or careers to consider. For Category One challenged spellers, spelling is an inconvenience, not a sentence.

At the opposite end of the continuum, Category Four, we find students who have no sense of personal control over language and who maintain little or no investment in their own literacy. They avoid the activities that are most apt to support growth in spelling skills, associating reading and writing with pain, not pleasure. Constant spelling errors have led to a sense of defeatism. These students cling to sound-it-out strategies and lament that "long" words or "hard" words leave them blank. Their external strategies—editors and spell checkers—place responsibility on the shoulders of others, if responsibility is placed at all. Most express the belief that spelling is unnecessary in the modern world and certainly not worth the trouble and frustration it has offered them.

Between these two extremes are students who lack information and sufficient strategies. As we revisit Figure 5–1, we see that the two middle categories reflect an erosion of literacy investment and sense of personal power. These students haven't given up on spelling—yet. Still, they clearly do not have the skills or the motivation they need to be able to work from a position of strength. Building upon what we know about challenged spellers, we must now ask ourselves, What do these challenged spellers need now to support their growth as writers, competence with spelling, and development of strategies for self-correction?

II

What Do Challenged Spellers Need?

I wish someone would just tell me how to do it. I mean, I'm tired of even thinking about spelling and I have to think about it all the time because I can never seem to remember words the right way. I'm always afraid my teachers will think I'm stupid or give me bad grades. What am I suppose to do?

JOSH

6

Confronting the Dilemma

Too much . . . too fast . . . too shallow: as we thought about reorienting our approach to teaching spelling in our classrooms, we did so with the realization that the revolving door of weekly lists, exercises, and tests had not been effective for the challenged spellers with whom we were working. In the best of scenarios, when those lists had represented patterns or rules or generalizations, these students had failed to adequately internalize that metacognitive information so that it could function as a tool for future application. In the worst of scenarios, when lists were simply collections of words that someone thought students should know, these students came away with the belief that every word in the language needs to be memorized individually—a task that they realized to be an impossibility.

We came to further realize that spelling instruction—even poor instruction—had generally stopped at the elementary school level. A number of our challenged spellers recollected this with relief. No longer were they burdened by struggling with a weekly list. Finally, they were able to shed their dread of the Friday test and the patina of failure that often accompanied it.

For much of our teaching careers, we, too, thought of spelling as a skill, a small part of the writing puzzle, and for us at the middle and high school levels, a seemingly insignificant skill at that. During our first years of teaching, we felt that spelling was unimportant. Karen explains, "I ignored spelling in my classroom because I felt that making meaning was much more important than helping students spell words. Besides, spelling was an elementary skill and one that a student should work on in a last draft." Karen shares this experience from one of her middle school classes that changed her mind:

> Kelly raised her hand. I called on her, knowing we were in for a treat as usual. She did not disappoint us. She took us on a galaxy journey using students in the

classroom and me as characters in her story. She was a natural writer. Her papers exploded with personality. If you ever wanted to show an example of voice, you would show one of Kelly's stories. After we were sitting back in our chairs and rubbing our bellies from laughter, the kids began to pack up. Kelly came up to me for my reaction.

"You're such a writer," I told her.

"No, I'm not," she refuted.

This again. Kelly would never admit that she could write. Every time a student had told her she was a good writer, she had refused the compliment. Today I asked her why she didn't believe she was a writer. She pointed at her paper.

"Yeah, I just heard it. You're incredible."

"But look at it." She held it close to my face.

I looked hard, trying to understand what she wanted me to see. There were spelling errors, but I could still read the words.

"I can't spell."

"Well, the spelling does need work. We'll work on editing it tomorrow."

"I can't write."

Kelly linked spelling with writing. She could not see it as a small part of writing. She saw spelling *as* writing. She felt embarrassed and did not want others to know about her spelling problems.

Our students helped us see that for those who struggle, spelling is not just an elementary skill; for many, it defines who they are as writers and as people. An experience in Dawn's high school classroom triggered this realization for her.

The bell rang and kids spilled noisily into the hallway. They slammed their lockers for the last time that school year, and yelling and laughing, they pushed their way out the doors into the bright summer sunlight. I let the noise interrupt the semester test grading I was supposed to be finishing. I was wishing I could be one of those carefree kids when Kathy, one of my sophomore writing students, appeared in my doorway.

"Are you busy?" she asked hesitantly.

"Grrrr . . . ," I growled as I plopped down a stack of papers dramatically. "Just a few more to go."

She laughed and walked into the room to stand near my desk.

"What's up?" I asked. "Shouldn't you be racing out of here like everyone else?"

"I wanted to see if you had graded mine yet." She pointed at the stack of papers in front of me.

I had read her semester test. As instructed, she wrote a query to a publisher and included a polished draft of the piece she wished to publish along with a self-addressed, stamped envelope. She had chosen her editorial, a thoughtful piece arguing that high school theatre groups should produce thought-provoking material and should not water down content in order to avoid controversy. The many examples Kathy included made her editorial very persuasive. She wrote with passion; however, she did not earn an A.

"It is right here," I said, digging her paper from the stack before me. I hesitated before I handed it to her. "It is really good, Kathy. You make some excellent points in your editorial. And I like how you really answer the opposing view. I just wish you had someone read it out loud to you before you turned it in. I think you could have caught some of your spelling mistakes."

"I know," she whispered, hanging her head, inspecting the floor at her feet.

"I mean, if you heard 'The issues that *plaque* our society can be addressed,' you could have fixed it."

She didn't answer. She didn't look up. I watched her swallow hard.

Please don't cry. I'm not saying that you're not smart, I thought. But I knew that was what she was hearing. That is what she had been hearing for the past nine years: *Other kids don't make these mistakes. Only stupid kids don't know how to spell.*

I handed the paper to her. She took it without looking at it.

"It is still a good paper, Kathy. You are a *good* writer."

"Thanks," she replied with no conviction.

Dawn came to realize that no matter what a student's strengths are, prevalent spelling errors can overshadow them all. Few mistakes are so glaring or so evident, so much so that they color the way a student perceives herself. These feelings of inadequacy and failure linked to poor spelling seemed to be engrained in many of our students. Tracy relates a familiar incident from her high school classroom:

> I crouched down next to Lori's desk, so we could speak at eye level. The room was quiet as students were reading their novels of choice. I handed Lori's latest paper back to her. The paper was full of comments and circled misspelled words. Lori looked at the misspelled words, and I could see her sink further into her chair. I meant to be positive with my comments and information by letting her know her spelling errors. I didn't take off one percentage point for each error, which was a way that many teachers in our school dealt with spelling problems.
>
> Instead of giving her a grade, I asked her to redo the paper. She looked at me as if a redo was worse than a failing grade. "I just can't write—I can't redo this," she mumbled as she peered at me with a look of desperation.
>
> "What do you mean you can't write? Your story is excellent. You just need to clean up the errors. That's the easy part." She stared at me in disbelief.
>
> "Just look at all of those errors. I just can't write," she insisted.
>
> It was then that it hit me. Lori equated spelling with writing.

Writing and spelling are inextricably intertwined for students like Kathy, Kelly, and Lori. Every word that our students struggle with is a struggle with writing, and the humiliation of getting back a piece of writing littered with words circled in red lingers with detrimental effect. While Category One or Two students (see Figure 5–1) tend to be able to delay concerns about spelling until final drafts, Lori and other students like her feel hopeless and cope by backing away from writing altogether. Poor spelling colors their perception of themselves as literacy learners.

Our students' feelings of inadequacy fueled our desire to find better methods for spelling instruction. As Karen explains,

> After talking with Kelly, and other students like her, I realized I needed to change. For me to teach only writing and reading was not enough for them. They weren't going to just pick [spelling] up after reading a few novels. They needed instruction. They needed some strategies that would help them while they wrote. They needed to hear that spelling was important because it helps their words and meanings come across clearly to their reader. They also needed to hear that spelling was only a small slice of the writing pie.

Because our goal was to help our students become capable and competent written communicators, we needed to find ways to empower students who equate their poor spelling with their writing and learning abilities. For Jennifer, this realization came from an experience with a parent.

> It was the night of student-led conferences. A mother and daughter sat hunched over the daughter's portfolio, giggling as she presented her work to her mom. After the excited eighth grader had finished explaining her best work to her mother, I slid my stool over to the front of the desks and began. "Your daughter is such a wonderful student. Everything she does is such high-quality work." The mom then gave an account of sports practices that left very little time for homework. The intricate plan the two of them had come up with for juggling homework was almost beyond anyone's comprehension, but it worked. As it was, the teen sat in her sport's uniform, here for the conference in between practices and lessons. "I would like her to pay closer attention to her spelling this year," I added.
>
> "It's my fault, I'm afraid," the mom mumbled.
>
> "All of my kids get it from me. It's hereditary—you know, bad spelling gene." I could tell she was embarrassed. "That's why I have this." She pulled a Franklin pocket speller out of her purse. "It's the least I can do for my kids, so each one of them gets one when they go off to college. I don't write anything without it."

A feeling of inadequacy as a speller had followed this woman around for years to the point where she felt guilty about passing on this inadequacy to her children. It was then that Jennifer realized how important it was to make sure that a student's sense of self-worth and intelligence wasn't clouded by the fact that she struggled with spelling.

Feelings of Apathy and Embarrassment

Besides feelings of inadequacy and failure as writers and students, challenged spellers must confront apathy. Like Kathy, Kelly, and Lori, these students feel as though spelling is beyond their control and, therefore, do little to correct their problems. For example, Ella is quick to admit that she is a poor speller and as quickly says that there is nothing she can do about it. She sees her poor spelling as a fault of the English language; it isn't her problem.

> I have a little problem with spelling. Wait, did I say a little problem? What I meant was that if the continuation of the human race depended on my spelling, you can count on being wiped out of existence. I've just never been the spelling type. Everything I write is phonetically spelled, and isn't that how it should be? Wouldn't the world make more sense if nothing with an *f* sound was spelled *ph* and *tion* was *shun?*"

Nancie has pretty much given up on spelling well:

> I can't spell. It's just as simple as that . . . Just two weeks ago I had to ask my mom how to spell *bowl*. First I tried "*bole*," didn't *loke* right, then "*boll*" looked pretty good, last I *scribled* down "*bool*" on the paper. Finally I gave up and asked my mom. I don't know if I spell *stupied*, weird, *tomarow*, or *colleage* right. I just don't know when I'm spelling them right or wrong. I don't think I'll ever be able to spell good, it's just a fact of life. I've accepted it and I'm moving on. So what if I spell at a fifth grade level. I still have my *prid*, oh *wiat*, *priid*, no *pirde*. Yeah, that's it.

Like Nancie and Ella, Nan doesn't see spelling as something she has power over. She learned to mask her poor spelling with bad handwriting because for her, as for many other students with spelling challenges, poor spelling is a source of embarrassment.

> Maybe I'll get over it, but it's not *some thing* I feel like I can change right now. The fact is it's really embarrassing and it is not cool to be in the advanced class but still feel dumb because I miss half of the spelling words at a sixth-grade level.

These students are not isolated cases. In one semester, out of thirty-nine advanced sophomore writing students in Dawn's classes, twelve students were spelling no higher than an eighth-grade level on the Richard Gentry Spelling Placement Test (Gentry 1997), and in many cases, these students with spelling difficulties were spelling at a sixth-grade level. Many of them felt the apathy that Ella, Nancie, and Nan described. Spelling, they think, is just something they do poorly, like some basketball players are poor free throwers. Unfortunately, many of these students do not believe that, like free throwing, spelling can be improved through continued use of appropriate strategies. The inadequacy, embarrassment, failure, and apathy felt by our challenged spellers, coupled with our frustration with traditional methods, pushed us to address spelling in more meaningful ways.

Core Understandings

Though challenged spellers often celebrated the end of spelling lists and tests, they desperately needed continued instruction with a broader emphasis on word and language study. In our settings, we found this possible only if we approached spelling strategically within the context of overall word awareness. Keenly aware that spelling is a writing skill, we decided the words we teach must have value in student writing. And to consider our instruction a success, we must be able to discern changes in student writing. It is one thing to see a change in grades on weekly tests; it is quite another to see words spelled correctly in final draft writing.

From our work with challenged spellers, a number of *core understandings* emerged; these now help shape our classroom practices (see Figure 6–1). In each case, the strategies and practices in these core understandings promote habits that extend beyond single words to clusters of words. These strategies are not add-ons in our day-to-day classroom work. Instead, they now are woven into the larger fabric of classroom instruction. Whether we are reading short stories or writing persuasive essays, these core understandings inform the entire curriculum from whole-class minilessons to small-group and/or individual conferences.

In order to be truly helpful to challenged spellers, instruction and strategies must
- promote reflection about spelling within the broader context of language study
- promote wordplay, word awareness, and investment in literacy
- generalize to groups of words to promote a sense of logic and order in the language
- support spelling of high-frequency words that students see and use often
- support the appropriate use of resources such as dictionaries, spell checkers, and editors
- support revision and editing through multiple drafts when correctness matters

Figure 6–1. Core Understandings About Supporting Challenged Spellers

Instead of focusing word study on exercises and tests, our core understandings promote reflection, wordplay, and concentration on skills that will help students in myriad writing situations. For students who already find themselves reluctant to read and write, equipping them with strategies and rules they can use in multiple settings is important, and language study should be an ongoing, enjoyable, and interesting part of our class instruction.

We want language and word awareness to be integral to everything that we do. As Jennifer so aptly says, our goal is to "marinate our students in language." In the following chapters, we provide examples of successful strategies we've used in order to reach this goal and offer glimpses into classrooms in which teachers articulate spelling and word study within the total context of their secondary curricula.

7

Promoting Reflection About Words

Helping students become more reflective about their spelling—learning to notice the quirks in their own spelling and to think about the reasons they struggle with particular words or kinds of words—offers them an opportunity to develop their own sense of power with language. Understanding that there are patterns to the errors they make and that they tend to experience difficulty with some types of words and not others helps free them from the notion that the entire language is beyond their control, that there is no logic that governs word formation. These strategies support the students in *thinking about their thinking*, in understanding why they are sometimes successful and other times unsuccessful, and how they can become in control more of the time.

Analyzing Their Own Writing

Helping students routinely analyze their own writing raises their awareness of the types of errors they make and helps them focus on particular kinds of words and strategies. As a college freshman, Josh has a long history as a challenged speller. Fortunately, he now exhibits an interest in gaining control over his spelling so that he can write more fluently. He produced the first draft shown in Figure 7–1 in his writing class (transcribed from handwritten copy).

When I first read Josh's paper, I was impressed with the sense of voice and purpose behind his words. He clearly communicates his frustration and his sense that an inequity exists. I read through the paper quickly with a yellow highlighter in hand, noting the words I found misspelled.

When Josh and I met to analyze his errors collaboratively using an error analysis chart (Figure 7–2), I first asked him to read his paper aloud to me and to pay particular attention to the words in yellow. He was able to identify quickly and

It was early on a Sunday morning. Four friends and I were driving back from MSU where we spent the night before when the unthinkable *happend*. We were only going 50 mph which is the speed *limet* when a police officer going the *oppisit* direction passes us and makes an abrupt *u-turn*. He starts to tail us about a mile *latter*. The driver, Don, one of my friends, makes a right turn at the next road. The police car *fallows* us and *emeditly* turns on his lights.

When the officer makes his way to the *drivers* side window he takes all of our licenses. After running them he comes back and tells the *drivers* to step out of the car. He then *surches* Don and puts him in the back of the police car. He then continues on to place all four of us into his car, in handcuffs. After we are locked in his car he continues on to *surch* the car. Before doing this he never read us our *meranda* rights or told us he was *planing* to *surch* the car.

At the end he found nothing in the car. After all of this he let us out of the car one at a time and took the handcuffs off. We never got an apology or a ticket to show his reason for this type of action.

How do *teen's* get treated differently by the law than other citizens and how can we stop that? There might not be *a* easy way to stop this problem unless you have lots of money. The way the law is set up you *cant* get back at them or *evean* say that it was an illegal *surch* or that you were *hurast* unless you hire a *layer* and you all know that that is expensive.

Figure 7–1. Josh's First Draft

independently the fact that he had chosen two wrong words (*latter* for *later* and *layer* for *lawyer*). For these he noted corrections directly on the paper. Two other words (*drivers* and *cant*) were equally easy to address. Josh admitted that he is sometimes forgetful about putting the apostrophe in a contraction and that he knows a possessive also requires an apostrophe. For two other words (*happend* and *planing*), he shrugged and admitted that he has lots of trouble remembering rules governing the addition of suffixes. We noted that on our conference sheet (Figure 7–3) for further work.

Our final two categories were clearly the ones for which we would need to devote instructional and conference time. As Josh pronounced each of the words in his paper, it was clear that association between sound and letters had created troublesome results for some of the words (see Figure 7–2). The repeated misspelling of *surch*, on the other hand, directed us to a specific pattern that he should review. Drawing Josh's attention to the fact that his pronunciation of words contributed to his misspellings helped him realize that he could eliminate

Student: Josh
Writing sample: "The Injustice of It All"
Total words: 295
Total incorrect: 15 different words   **Total duplicates:** 3

Homophones/wrong words	Structural and pronunciaton concerns
latter (later)	*limet* (limit)
layer (lawyer)	*oppisit* (opposite)
	fallows (follows)
	emeditly (immediately)
Faulty grammatical knowledge	*evean* (even)
drivers (driver's)	*meranda* (Miranda)
cant (can't)	*surches* (searches)
a (an)	*surch* (search)
	surch (search)
	surch (search)
Prefix/suffix errors	*hurast* (harassed)
happend (happened)	
planing (planning)	
	Incorrect splitting or joining words

Figure 7–2. Josh's Error Analysis Chart

Student: Josh
Date: September '01
Writing sample: "The Injustice of It All"
Notes for study:
1. Read papers aloud carefully, listening to each word to be sure sounds and letters match.
2. Remember to double the final consonant in a single-syllable word ending in a consonant before adding *-ing*.
3. In a word like *search* where the *ea* is combined with the *r* to make a "ur" sound, what can we do to remember the *ea*? [Josh decided on a mnemonic device: "I'll search the sea for clues!"]
4. Add any of the words from the analysis to your personal dictionary if you think you'll need a reminder.

Figure 7–3. Josh's Spelling Conference Log

many problem words by slowing down, breaking words into sound chunks, and listening carefully to syllables.

As we talked about his paper, Josh and I kept notes in a spelling conference log (Figure 7–3). We agreed that he would practice reading his papers aloud, listening to all the words, but particularly to words with which he tended to have difficulty. We also noted a need to revisit rules for adding suffixes and talked specifically about rules governing the addition of -ed and -ing.

Because I had worked with Josh for some time, I knew that he tended to have difficulty with visual memory. Because of this, he needed strategies that aren't totally dependent on visual recall. Earlier I'd shared with him that I'd had to look up the word *accommodate* every time I used it for years until someone told me I would need to accommodate the twins: two *c*s and two *m*s. That's all it took. In the past Josh had experienced success using mnemonic devices as well. He decided to create a mnemonic device for *search* and came up with "I'll search the sea" (see Figure 7–3).

Conferencing with Josh on his error analysis took about five minutes. Part of that time was spent helping him see that he already knew a great deal about spelling. For example, even though he misspelled *search* (*es*) four times, he had already learned to use the *-es* suffix correctly following a *-ch* ending. His ability to self-correct four words and understand that four other errors could be addressed by adding one strategy to his repertoire meant that he had seven words to focus on, not fifteen. It also helped me isolate a few specific skills to focus on in future minilessons and conferences. By maintaining a journal log, we were able to track his areas of focus across the semester, a strategy that helped both of us approach his spelling needs more strategically.

Personal Spelling Dictionaries and Lists

Josh maintains a personal spelling dictionary of words he tends to misspell. So do other students in our classes. The ways these dictionaries are constructed vary from class to class. In my class, I ask students to keep words on pages in the back of their response logs. In Jennifer's class, a section in the language arts notebook is set up for that purpose. In most cases, personal dictionaries include straightforward information such as that found in the excerpt from Josh's dictionary in Figure 7–4.

Because Josh tends to repeat some types of errors frequently, we often transfer several highly problematic words to a five-by-seven-inch card to place by his computer or in the front of his notebook. He gives those target words particular attention for a few weeks. Much like my own solution with *accommodate*, focused attention and the creation of a personal strategy generally bring the words under control, at which point new target words replace them.

Correctly spelled word	Likely misspellings
search	surch
searches	surches

Figure 7–4. Josh's Personal Spelling Dictionary

Personal spelling lists are integral to Karen's overall approach to teaching spelling at the middle school level. Each of her students has a chart where he or she writes down words he or she has misspelled in a final draft or words he or she misspells repeatedly and wants to learn. The list is cumulative, and Karen collects it every time a student turns in a close-to-final draft or portfolio. She is able to make sure students have spelled the problem words correctly in their drafts, and she can circle new ones to be added, though she limits these to five words. These lists help students remain conscious of their own spelling challenges. Karen works with students on an individual basis to teach and reinforce strategies that help them remember how to spell those personally challenging words. These lists also function as a resource to students, providing a quick reference for spelling the words that are most troublesome for them. To raise student awareness even more, Karen often asks students to put a check in the margin of their papers when they have used one of their own personal spelling list words.

Using Reflection Logs

We've found various types of spelling logs useful for focusing students' attention on their typical errors. For example, in the fall, Jennifer makes sure each of her middle school students has a section in his or her language arts binder devoted to spelling. By creating a spelling log like the one in Figure 7–5, students think about the words they misspelled and why they misspelled them.

Jennifer lists in the lower left-hand corner of each corrected draft words the student misspelled, focusing on one or two words at a time. The first thing students do when a draft is returned is check out their problem words. In their spelling logs, they record the correct spelling of each word and a reflection on why they misspelled it (error analysis). Jennifer encourages students to think about their spelling process, placing emphasis on student ownership; she expects

Correct spelling of the word:
Why do you think you
    misspelled the word?
What kind of word is it?

Figure 7–5. Spelling Log from Jennifer's Class

Spelling Log

Student name:

Misspelled Word   Correct Spelling   Error Analysis

_____   _____   _____

Strategy to try:

Figure 7–6a. Spelling Log from Dawn's Class

her middle schoolers to think about their typical errors and apply new information in future writing. In the third part of the entry, students are asked to think about characteristics of the words they misspelled: For example, was the word a homophone? Was it an *i* before *e* except after *c* word? Students maintain their logs throughout the year and revisit them often. Logs become artifacts for discussion during student-teacher conferences as well as conferences with parents.

Dawn's spelling log for her high school students (Figures 7–6a and 7–6b) is slightly different from Jennifer's. When Dawn returns a final draft, she asks, "What mistakes were made? Do you see any patterns in your mistakes? What can you do to avoid these mistakes the next time?" She asks her high school students to take an active role in thinking about and categorizing their own errors. By using reflective strategies over time, students establish the habit of thinking about their spelling rather than just filing the paper away and hoping for better results in the future. They become strategic—as do we as teachers—in thinking about the types of errors they make and ways of addressing them.

Spelling Log

Misspelled Word	Correct Spelling	Error Analysis
strait	straight	homophones

Strategy to try _Have a go_

Misspelled Word	Correct Spelling	Error Analysis
write	right	homophones

Strategy to try _mnemonic devices_

If you have a will to write then spell it w/ a W !

Misspelled Word	Correct Spelling	Error Analysis
then	Than	homophone

Strategy to try _mnemonic devices_

Misspelled Word	Correct Spelling	Error Analysis
inapropriate	Inappropriate	double letter

Strategy to try _have a go_

Figure 7–6b. Devon's Spelling Log from Dawn's Class

Spelling Log

Misspelled Word	Correct Spelling	Error Analysis
to	two	homophones

Strategy to try <u>mnemonic device</u>

if you are talking about more than one thing then it has the extra letter. (w)

Misspelled Word	Correct Spelling	Error Analysis
priorady	priority	spelled the way it sounds instead of real way

Strategy to try <u>visualization</u>

Misspelled Word	Correct Spelling	Error Analysis
occured	occurred	double letter

Strategy to try <u>have a go</u>

Misspelled Word	Correct Spelling	Error Analysis

Strategy to try _____

Figure 7–6b. (*continued*)

8

Less but Deeper
Teaching Strategies and Rules That Generalize

To provide deeper opportunities for our students to learn information about words that will generalize to other words, we make use of a variety of strategies that are ongoing parts of our classroom structure. Many of the reflective strategies that promote word awareness are ones that have a natural place in our classrooms. Word walls, literature circle word study, human words, card sorts, and investigation into spelling rules all provide opportunities for students to think about how a particular feature may be useful in remembering the spelling of many different words.

Word Walls

Building word walls is one effective technique for encouraging word study. Whether we are looking for words that reflect a particular principle, words that illustrate clusters of synonyms, or words that build vocabulary for particular types of content-specific writing, word walls are interesting ways to engage students in active participation through finding and displaying words. What types of word walls have we found effective? Figure 8–1 offers a glimpse at the variations we have used.

In Karen's classroom, an alphabetical word wall is hung around the room from the very beginning of the school year and features words that are frequently used and frequently misspelled. The words *poem, know, there, congratulations, tomorrow,* and *sincerely* might be examples of words on this list. On another list Karen places signal cards next to homophones; these help students know which word is actually spelled a particular way. For instance, *no* might be up on the wall with the signal card *yes* right next to it to let students know it is the word that means an answer, not the word that refers to thinking or recognizing a person.

In Karen's class, words are added to the word wall when students bring them up in class or when a word is frequently misspelled in a majority of papers. Though

- words that illustrate a particular rule, like doubling a final consonant when adding *-ing* in words like *plan/planning*, *ban/banning*, *can/canning* or using a silent *e* in single-syllable words that reflect a CVC pattern, like *rule* and *cute*
- clusters of words that take the place of tired, overworked words like *nice*, *good*, and *happy*
- words that build from a common root, like *-spect* building to *inspect*, *inspection*, *prospect*, *introspect*, *spectrograph*, and others
- words associated with a theme we are exploring in our literature, in a content-related interdisciplinary unit, or in our writing (For example, when reading about diversity, we might build a wall filled with words associated with racism, sexism, individualism, and class differences. When reading *Harry Potter*, we might look for words we've found in the text or words associated with magic that we find in other types of print.)
- words that give students the most trouble along with tips for spelling them

Figure 8–1. Types of Word Walls

some word walls are teacher- and student-generated, others come from published sources. For example, Carson-Dellosa Publishers provides a handy collection of high-use words and homophones that Karen draws from at the onset of the school year. Words are on a blue background and appear in shape boxes to help students visualize the way each word looks. As the year progresses, she simply adds to the list other words that seem to give her students continuous trouble.

Karen is able to help students focus on new words that have suddenly become high-use words in content area study. Since Karen teaches in a team, she often includes words students have problems with in other classes, too. Because content-related words are often also new words for students, she links the words thematically. This helps students make meaning as they easily access the new words for inclusion in their writing. The back bulletin board in Karen's classroom functions as a thematic word wall. When students are engaged in their integrated study of the moon, for example, that month's word wall features moon-related words such as *lunar*, *waxing*, *waning*, and *illuminate*. When they are engaged in a study of poetry, the language arts word wall includes words such as *simile*, *metaphor*, and *personification* as new focuses for study. Clearly, this bridges spelling and vocabulary development across the curriculum.

Organization of the word walls is very important if they are to be effective tools for students who are looking for particular words. It is too confusing to have words just placed anywhere within the classroom. Karen makes a heading for each group of words and classifies them in the correct columns or alphabetically so her students can find the words easily when they are writing. For example, under the letter *B*, Karen might include problem words such as *basement*, *beautiful*, *beginning*, *bibliography*, *blockade*, and *break*. The more practice students get at spelling a word correctly, the more they will improve.

The word wall shown in Figure 8–2 serves multiple purposes for Dawn's high school students. Because she has chosen to develop it with different colors of Post-it Notes, she is able to ask students to provide information about each of the words they add to the wall. In this case, colors stand for various parts of speech. As a word is considered, students note its use and choose the appropriate color for it.

Poetry Walls

Poetry walls are a natural extension of word walls. Filling walls with interesting words invites the creation of "motion" poetry, formed by manipulating the words available on the wall. For example, when studying nature writing, I pass out Post-it Notes to students, asking each of them to bring in five to ten interesting words, phrases, or clusters of words to add to our word wall bank. Words may be selected from published materials or may be ones students think about as they observe nature settings. Students work individually or in small groups selecting words from the word wall bank to rearrange into poems that are left up for a day or two before they are rearranged into new poems. These motion poems are made richer by the constant replenishing of new words. In Dawn's classroom, where words are coded by their part of speech, this activity reinforces the appropriate use of a rich array of vocabulary words. Clearly, motion poetry places a focus on words, promotes play with language, and breaks down barriers to poetry for reluctant readers and writers. Continuously revisiting words helps students focus on both spelling and meaning.

Other possibilities for word walls are endless. For example, word walls can be set up as graffiti boards on which students simply write or attach words that they find in environmental print, newspapers, books they are reading, and materials from other content area classes. Playful competition among groups to find particular types of words and to create poems that other students enjoy serves as a great motivator for students to search for words in all kinds of places.

Human Words

After teaching a rule, pattern, or generalization, Jennifer encourages her students to engage in active learning by asking them to help create "human words." For example, after teaching the silent *e* rule, she passes out a letter card—a piece of

Figure 8–2. Word Wall from Dawn's Classroom

construction paper with an individual letter written on it—to each student in the class. When she calls out a word, students who have the letters in the word stand at the front of the classroom and arrange themselves in the proper order to spell the word correctly. For example, if she calls out *slide*, all students with one of those letters come to the front of the room to spell S-L-I-D-E. Then if she calls out *sliding*, the students, particularly the one holding the silent *e*, must decide whether to stay or to go when the suffix is added.

Active participation is the important factor in human words. This activity encourages thinking about words, reflecting on the use of a rule or pattern, and making decisions about the application of a rule or pattern; and, since middle schoolers have a tough time sitting still all period, the movement creates an interesting way to promote reflection and learning.

Literature Circles

Many of us have tried literature circles, or a variation of them, in our classes. As described by Daniels (1994), literature circles support focused discussion through the use of assigned roles. Frequently, one of our literature circle roles encourages students to focus on new words, interesting words, or words used in unusual ways in their reading. The word wizard role, for example, helps students think not just about new words or hard words but also about interesting ways everyday words are used by good authors. We've found that the more our challenged spellers look at words and think about them, the more they are likely to develop investment in words in their own writing.

This continuous search for words sometimes extends beyond our reading to awareness of environmental print. Trips to the grocery store, time spent with a favorite magazine, and routine correspondence all offer opportunities to rediscover words as they are being used in innovative ways. We make time to talk about quirky and interesting uses of language in our classes, and, yes, these words often make their way on to word walls or graffiti boards. As noted earlier, we want to marinate the students in language in everything that we do.

Card Sorts

Both Karen and Jennifer work with inductive reasoning strategies in their middle school classes. Karen has found it really effective to create decks of cards from which students study clusters of words to determine the governing pattern or rule that is represented by each of the words in the deck. Students find it liberating when they can figure out the rules that make words work and are able to own those rules and transfer them to new words.

Karen gives small groups of students stacks of three-by-five-inch cards with words written on them. Each stack represents one spelling rule or pattern. Students examine the words, investigate how they are spelled, and determine what makes them similar. Groups then compose a rule using a complete sentence that explains the common feature of the words. For example, one stack of cards might contain words like the following:

nice	nicest
cute	cutest
state	statement

These words ending in silent *e* are ones in which the *e* is kept when a suffix beginning with a consonant is added.

After the groups have determined the rules, they put the rules and sample words on poster paper to display on the wall. They add additional words to their posters that fit the rules they have discovered. This way, the students are surrounded by words and the logic behind their spelling. By thinking about words together and making decisions about the type of spelling pattern or rule at work, students develop ownership for their knowledge of the pattern and may then extend application of that knowledge beyond the words given to identify new words that reflect it. For challenged spellers, engagement with spelling in a fun setting with words that are accessible creates the opportunity for them to feel successful. Resources for other spelling activities are annotated in Appendix L, including *Words Their Way* (Bear et al. 2000), which contains a trove of information on word sorts.

Rules Worth Knowing

The secondary school day overflows with important things to do. For strategies or rules to be worth our instructional time, they must help students internalize patterns or rules that generalize to other applications. In so doing, students can focus not only on those situations where the rules and patterns hold but on the exceptions as well.

Challenged spellers need rules that work most of the time (see Figure 8–3). Students need time to experiment with words for which these rules work as well as with words that are exceptions to the rules. Teaching a narrowly applied definition, as Dan described earlier regarding the application of the *-ly* rule, leaves challenged spellers in no better shape than they were before the lesson began.

Despite the fact that there are exceptions to most rules that govern English spelling, a few rules are worth the time and effort of reteaching because of their

Rules for prefixes

Generally when a prefix is added to a word, do not drop a letter from either the base word or the prefix (*dis* + *approve* = *disapprove*). Exceptions include *ad-*, *com-*, and *in-*, which can be absorbed by the base word so that the last letter in the prefix changes to match the beginning consonant of the base word (as in *illegal* instead of *inlegal*).

Rules for *i* before *e*

Write *i* before *e* (*fiery*, *friend*) except after *c* or when sounded like *a* as in *neighbor* and *weigh*. When the *ie* or *ei* is not pronounced *ee*, it is usually spelled *ei* (*reign*).

Rules for plurals

When forming the plural of most words, just add *s*.

When forming the plural of a word that ends with a *y* that is preceded by a vowel, add *s* (as in *monkeys*, *turkeys*).

When forming the plural of a word that ends in an *o* that is preceded by a vowel, add *s* (as in *patio/patios*).

When forming the plural of a word that ends in an *o* that is preceded by a consonant, add *es* (as in *tomato/tomatoes*).

Rules for suffixes

When a one-syllable word ends in a consonant preceded by one vowel, double the final consonant before adding a suffix that begins with a vowel (as in *run/running*).

In a word with two or more syllables that ends with a consonant-vowel-consonant, double the final letter before adding a suffix beginning with a vowel if the final syllable is stressed (as in *commit/committed*). If the final syllable is not stressed, do not double the final letter (as in *cancel/canceled*, *blanket/blanketed*).

If a word ends with a silent *e*, drop the *e* before adding a suffix that begins with a vowel (as in *give/giving*, *take/taking*).

When adding a suffix to a word where *y* is the last letter in a word and the *y* is preceded by a consonant, change the *y* to *i* before adding any suffix except those beginning with *i* (as in *happy/happiness*, *happily*).

When adding the suffix *-ly* or *-ness*, do not change the spelling of the base word unless it ends in *y* (*careful/carefully*, *fond/fondness*, *gay/gaily*).

Figure 8–3. Rules Worth Knowing

-*ible* and -*able*

If a root is not a complete word, add -*ible* (as in *visible, edible, illegible*).

If a root is a complete word, add -*able* (as in *suitable, dependable, workable*).

If a root is a complete word that ends in a silent *e*, drop the *e* and add -*able* (as in *advisable, likable, valuable*).

Exceptions to the -*ible/-able* rule occur when the final sound is the hard *g* or *c*. Then the suffix used is -*able* (as in *apply/applicable*).

-*ion*

If the root ends in *ct*, add -*ion* (as in *select/selection*).

If the root ends in *ss*, add -*ion* (as in *discussion/discussion*).

If the root ends in *te*, drop the *e* and add -*ion* (as in *educate/education*).

If the root ends in *it*, change the *t* to *s* and add -*ion* (as in *permit/permission*).

If the root ends in *vowel-d-e*, drop the *e*, change the *d* to *s* and add -*ion* (as in *explode/explosion*).

Note: see Appendix J for additional resources

Figure 8–3. (*continued*)

high level of reliability. When offering instruction in spelling rules, Karen reminds us that less is better. We focus on six rules, shown in Figure 8-3, and provide plenty of time for students to play with words that fit each one. If we have time, or if students demonstrate a need, we extend beyond these to rules that are less in demand or that work less consistently.

Jennifer reminds us that it's "imperative to give middle school students the same information about fifty times and in fifty ways"—good advice at almost any level. Students told us repeatedly that they were unsuccessful when bombarded with too much, too fast, and strategies that were too narrow, so Jennifer teaches spelling rules slowly, sometimes covering no more than two rules by Thanksgiving, and draws upon visual strategies like word walls, kinesthetic strategies like human words, and other strategies that require the active involvement of students.

Jennifer displays rules prominently on a bulletin board so they constantly surround students. She keeps a word wall in the back of the room as well, covered with all the words they have worked on. Word cards and posters fill her room. Karen's classroom is filled with word walls that illustrate particular spelling patterns or rules. The idea is to immerse our students in language, to intrigue and tease them with words.

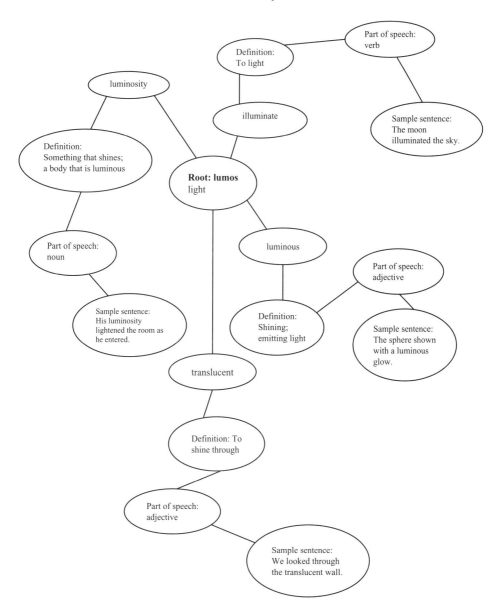

Figure 8–4. Word Web

Karen, Jennifer, Tracy, and Dawn all spend time with challenged spellers discussing roots, suffixes, and prefixes. And, though visual aids for thinking about the ways words are built vary, Figure 8–4 illustrates one type of device we use: a word web. Jennifer describes how the root *lumos* came to interest her students after reading *Harry Potter*. From *lumos* as a root, students generated *luminous*, *illuminate*, *illuminated*, and finally, *luminosity*.

Karen says her students seem comforted by the knowledge that words build on and from each other—that if they know one root, it will help them know and spell many others. She presented *aud* (to hear) and sent students on a search for words that related to this base. They found words like *auditorium*, *audible*, *audience*, and *audio*; then individuals or small groups created word webs on poster paper. Posters were hung around the room as tools for spelling and as encouragement to try out new vocabulary in their writing.

In these examples, each strategy is intended to be built upon over the course of an entire semester or year. Instead of jumping from one spelling activity to another, each of these strategies is intended to provide a deep structure that can function unobtrusively as a platform for word study within middle and high school settings. To be successful, they must be built, rebuilt, and adapted so that students absorb a metacognitive sense about their language.

As teachers of challenged spellers, our own excitement about words is supremely important. When we highlight words from our own reading, display our own curiosity about words, put words up on the board for students to examine and question, and encourage students to weave those words into their own writing, we are helping them begin to see that language is rich, interesting, and fun rather than something that is always academic, testable, and painful.

9

Focusing on Other Supporting Strategies

Concentrating on High-Frequency Words

While there is clearly a bridge between vocabulary and spelling development—particularly when working with roots, suffixes, and prefixes—learning to spell is sometimes made more complicated for challenged spellers when they are asked to master the spelling of words that they would rarely use in writing. For example, in Anchorage a number of years ago, one of the seventh-grade spelling word lists contained the word *mezzanine*. My students looked at me quizzically. "What's a *mezzanine?*" their eyes asked, a legitimate question. At that time there were few buildings with mezzanines in the entire state, so my students had little experience with one and wouldn't be apt to use the word *mezzanine* their writing. It is an unfortunate reality that published spelling texts, in efforts to teach a particular rule or pattern, often include words that are unfamiliar and unlikely to be used in order to have enough words to fill a list. Of course, we want to encourage students to stretch their vocabularies—and there are appropriate ways to do so—but when a student struggles routinely with high-use words, it makes sense to concentrate attention on these words as priorities.

While the English language contains more than 750,000 words, and continues to grow each year, a mere 1,000 words make up about 90 percent of the words used in routine written communication (Horn 1926). These words are so essential to writing that we would find it impossible to write without them (see Figure 9–1). Remarkably, the list of high-frequency words has changed very little since Horn's original list was compiled: "Less than 4 per cent of these words have come into the language since 1849, and less than 10 per cent have come in since 1749. More of these words were in the language before 1099 than have come into the language since 1799" (Horn 1939, 134). Moreover, standard English high-frequency words

- 1,000 words: 90 percent of routine written communication
- 2,000: 95.3 percent of routine written communication
- 3,000: 97.6 percent of routine written communication
- 4,000: 98.7 percent of routine written communication
- 5,000: 99.2 percent of routine written communication

Figure 9–1. High-Frequency Word Facts

do not seem to fluctuate according to geographic location within the United States, which allows teachers to comfortably draw from the high-frequency lists that are readily available.

According to Horn, the most important 1,000 words are used an average of nine times as often as other words. Without the ability to spell about 3,000 high-frequency words at a level of automaticity, writers are forced to spend far too much time looking up words, searching for substitute words, and seeking various types of help.

So what are the high-frequency words our students should know? In the first 100 most used words, we find ones that most of us encountered in the primary grades. These include words like *a, all, am, are, as, I'm, if, is, our, up, us, very, what,* and *your.* Certainly, most of our secondary and college students have mastered these words by the time they reach our classes. However, as we move up the list of even the first 1,000 high-frequency words, we find words like the ones shown in Figure 9–2 that, though used repeatedly in everyday writing, are often still problematic for many of our students. (See Appendix I.)

There is an important distinction to remember when working with high-frequency lists: these lists are very different from the lists of the most frequently misspelled words found in many writing handbooks. The most often misspelled words are, of course, the ones with which most of us struggle. These lists include words such as those shown in Figure 9–3.

While we readily grant that these are important words to know, starting with lists of these words may cause some challenged spellers to throw up their hands in complete and utter frustration.

In addition to working with high-frequency words identified from established lists, such as those by Pinnell and Fountas (1998) and Sitton (1995), we've found it important to pay careful attention to high-frequency words representative of a student's writing. By the time students are in the secondary grades, they are likely to have developed strong patterns of interest that will embrace specialized vocabulary, which becomes high frequency for them. By helping students look closely at the words they misspell and, through this process, identify words that

average	*tomorrow*	*they're*
climbed	*potatoes*	*receive*
sincerely	*bicycle*	*knife*
fifty	*threw*	*spelling*
swimming	*mistake*	*actually*
muscles	*dictionary*	*ordinary*
pencil	*lose*	*vegetable*
altogether	*although*	*disease*
motor	*daughter*	*success*
waste	*foreign*	*rhythm*
recommend	*factory*	*principal*
college	*barbecue*	*accident*
(Sitton 1995, 82)		

Figure 9–2. Sample High-Frequency Words

are high frequency within their own writing, we are able to generate a personalized cluster of words for special attention.

What strategies work for teaching high-frequency words? Two types of strategies are important: ones that help with the skill of spelling and ones that help the students become more reflective, building their own metacognitive powers over language. Challenged spellers require many opportunities to look at and reflect upon high-frequency words. For example, high-frequency word lists may be taped to desks, placed in high-frequency personal dictionaries, or added to wall charts for whole-class emphasis. Gail Thibodeau (2002, 19–21) describes a schoolwide project that involved identifying and creating lists of "unforgivables," or words that all students should know at each grade level. Once these words were identified and agreed upon, teachers in English and other content areas expected students to spell these words correctly every time. Constant exposure to these words and consistent reinforcement of them across the curriculum increased the chance that challenged spellers would focus on them.

accommodate	*achievement*	*acquire*
all right	*among*	*apparent*
comparative	*conscious*	*disastrous*
exaggerate	*explanation*	*fascinate*

Figure 9–3. Most Frequently Misspelled Words

High-frequency homophones are a special concern. As a middle school teacher, Jennifer focuses her students' attention on these by giving each student a one-inch binder ring onto which the student attaches three-by-five-inch cards with a hole punched in the corner (see Figure 9–4). She begins with three of the most troublesome homophones for her students: *their, there,* and *they're.* Since problems with these are so widespread, each student writes the words, short definitions, and example sentences on his or her card. Each student then strings the cards on his or her binder ring and closes it around a ring of his or her language arts binder. One card is added each week or two focusing on different homophones. Students are expected to use the cards as a quick reference tool, and Jennifer insists that they not mix up the homophones again in their writing (see Appendix K for a list of frequently confused homophones).

Once problem words are identified, students should be encouraged to draw upon every spelling strategy they have learned. Mnemonics such as the one described earlier to help spell *accommodate* are useful. Similarly, some students find it useful to make up jingles to help them remember words. For example, one student recalled that his teacher in an earlier grade had told him to remember "George Efird's old goat ran a pig home yesterday" to spell *geography* and, for *arithmetic,* "A rat in Tom's house might eat Tom's ice cream." Silly? Of course! But these mnemonic devices help us remember words and free us of the burden of looking them up.

Most of us have drawn upon some type of visualization strategy to help students remember high-frequency words as well. These strategies may be as simple as having a student create a picture or drawing with the words to help him remember their shape or enhance parts of words to make him more aware of the parts he tends to misspell. In Dawn's high school classroom, students create visuals such as the ones in Figure 9–5 and are surrounded by these colorful reminders of the correctly spelled words. These visualizations make great resources to add to our word art posted around the classroom.

Many students describe putting words to music or rhythms. Still others remember by drawing on kinesthetic strengths. For Josh, one kinesthetic strategy involves tracing a word in the palm of his hand with a finger from the other hand; for others, tracing a word in sand or on soft fabric helps reinforce the shape and feel of a word.

High-frequency words provide challenged spellers with a wonderful opportunity to use reflective practices. Maintaining spelling logs or journals helps challenged spellers think about the types of words they tend to misspell, why they tend to misspell them, and what they can do to prevent misspelling them in the future. To heighten their awareness, they might begin searching for their high-frequency words in newspapers, magazines, and books; in ads and in environmental print; and

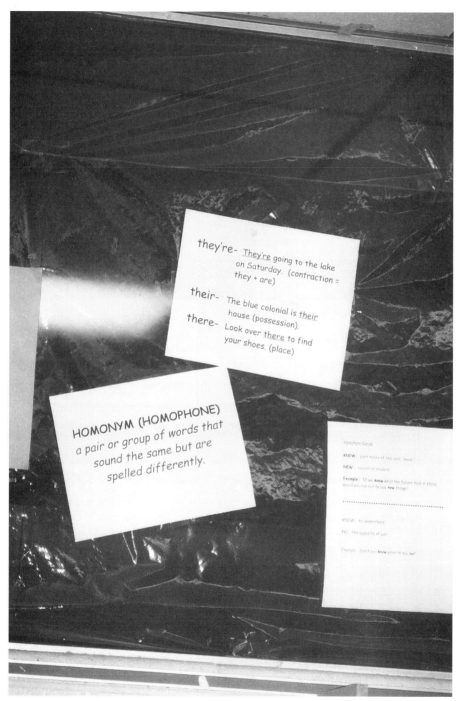

Figure 9–4. Jennifer's Homophone Cards

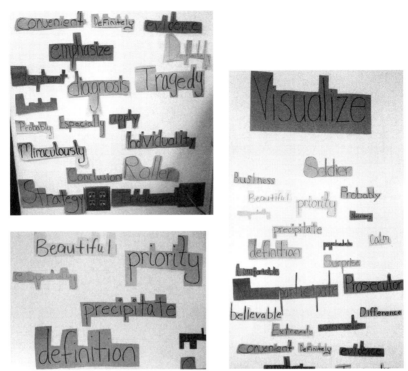

Figure 9–5. Word Pictures

in their own writing. If they are to remember troublesome high-frequency words, it is imperative that they use them often in their own writing. Doing so consciously and placing a check in the margin when they do helps the writers and the teacher take note of the word being spelled correctly.

Using External Resources Appropriately

Challenged spellers use external tools like dictionaries minimally. Jay, a high school student, described the phenomenon: "Just look it up? I don't get when people say this. How do you look it up if you don't know how to spell it?" Jay, like most of our other student collaborators, could not remember being instructed in how a dictionary can be used to find the correct spelling of words. However, teaching students to identify and find the first syllable of a word and search from there could demonstrate a use for dictionaries and reinforce a sense of power and independence. Many adults keep books such as *Webster's Instant Word Guide* on their desks. This type of book lists high-use words in syllables without definitions or any other information—a quick and easy resource.

Reading aloud is perhaps the simplest and most overlooked strategy to support editing. We explain to students that their brain processes faster than either their eyes or their hands. The brain can easily substitute words, add words, or delete words as the eyes scan along in silent reading. When we read aloud—and read exactly what is on the paper—we force ourselves to see and hear exactly what we have written. Doing so and listening to the sound of the piece will generally help students hear when an incorrect substitution—like *choose* for *chose* and *pubic* for *public*—has occurred. Errors seem to jump off the page at us as we read, "I walked *or* the place *were* you described."

Almost everyone loves spell checkers. However, challenged spellers—indeed, all spellers—need to know that spell checkers can really lead them into trouble. Depending on the importance of the text being generated, a spell-checked draft should first be read aloud by the writer and then shared with an editor. The use of editors for important drafts has become a more common practice in writing process–oriented classrooms. Peer editors, teacher conferences, and editing stations all provide opportunities for students to benefit from another set of eyes. Students often find it reassuring to know that all published writing moves through the capable hands of a copy editor. Used appropriately, external editing of a publication-quality final draft models the process "real" writers go through and gives teachers additional opportunities to help students focus reflectively on the words that are most troublesome for them.

Thinking of Spelling as a Process

Years ago, writing was approached very differently than it is today. Many of us moved through school with little notion of the processes we drew upon to write successfully in various genres. Today, building upon decades of research on writing, teachers have a much clearer picture of the complexity of the process that takes place for each writer as she moves from need to idea to product. As we have worked with both able spellers and challenged spellers in our classrooms, we have come to understand that the role of process in spelling is a huge consideration. Just as proficient readers and writers have internalized a process for approaching new tasks, proficient spellers have done the same. For many, however, their process for spelling problem words may be so unexamined they are unaware of its existence.

Writing begins with a foundational knowledge base. Writers have stored information about language mechanics that ranges from the fact that our written language is presented in a left-to-right fashion across the page to the fact that thought segments are generally set off by capital letters at the beginning and end punctuation at the end. If their knowledge base is complete enough, they know some things about the genre in which they plan to write. How are thoughts expressed in this genre? Should the writer use facts, similes, metaphors, or other figurative uses of language? How are the words and paragraphs supposed to look on the page? Genre suggests specificity, and writers need to know the specifics of a genre if they are to become successful in that genre.

All of this speaks to baseline knowledge. It still does not ensure that a writer will write successfully, nor does it guarantee that the words he puts on the page will be of sufficient interest or appeal to a reader to make them worth reading. Beyond knowledge, there are other considerations that writers must think about in the process of writing, and these include very important features like organization, fluency, vocabulary, and voice. If we choose to think of spelling as a process, we begin to frame our thinking about spelling in terms of how we correctly spell words in authentic writing situations. Spelling as a process operates at two levels: the production of written text and the development of a correctly spelled written vocabulary.

Clearly, deciding upon what our message will be is as important as its clear expression on paper or on a computer screen. For example, when working with expository text, part of the research process must address the technical vocabulary necessary to the piece. In the act of reading and researching, the writer creates a store of essential words for writing about the content in the selected genre.

As writers move into drafting the piece, they may choose to delay concerns about correct spelling until the draft takes shape. While in its formative stage, they may not want to reduce the flow of ideas by stopping to spell a word. Instead, they may decide in advance to write a close approximation for uncertain words or even to leave a blank to come back to later.

Revision is no longer a process of tweaking the final draft as a whole. For many, revision starts after the second sentence and continues in tight sentence- and paragraph-level rereadings as they carefully waltz through the piece. During this revision, spelling is secondary to word choice as writers strive to communicate with the most effective words possible.

Editing decisions have everything to do with purpose and audience. If the piece is important, if it is going to a critical audience, or if the purpose behind the writing is important to us, editing takes on added significance. When the writing is high stakes, writers need a spelling process in place that they can rely upon.

How do writers edit for spelling? Precisely because the answer is highly subjective, it is important to think about. When writers have no notion of their own writing process, each new writing venture is filled with mystery. To identify process, writers ask themselves questions. How did I go about creating that successful paper last time? Are there parts of the process that I can draw upon predictably? Writers have individual and idiosyncratic writing processes, and successful writers all have a spelling process as well. If writers are conscious of that process and use it in a consistent manner, the process becomes a tool. They can use it to help spell words correctly as they write and to help them add words to their repertoire for use later. For example, as a young writer, my own process for spelling was sorely limited. Since I did not have a particularly strong visual memory, I often found myself struggling to remember words that I had seen in other texts. And, since I was unaware of the strategy of using a placeholder or a word approximation until later, the flow of my writing generally stopped while I looked up words in a dictionary. As a young writer, I knew little about the concept of multiple drafts. As a result, I wanted to keep the writing as clean as possible so editing for a final copy would be easier.

How different that is from my process now, which itself fluctuates depending on whether my work is word processed or handwritten. Using my word processor, I have the advantage of the little red line that appears beneath misspelled words. Many times I will click on the word and clean up the spelling immediately. If, however, I'm experiencing a real flow in the writing, I won't stop for anything until the ideas are down and saved. What happens when the text is handwritten? Again, purpose and audience are paramount. If I'm handwriting in my journal, I'll keep going. On the other hand, if the writing will be going to another reader, I generally stop to use my *Instant Word Guide*. If that's unavailable and no other resources are there, I'll use a different word.

It irritates me to look up the same word time after time, so I also have a process for remembering words. I selectively focus my attention on a word or two that particularly trouble me. Why do I stumble on the word *schedule*? What parts of the word trip me up? Once these are identified, I select a strategy to help me remember the word. This time my cue is visual: I visualize the word in three parts, with *sch* at one end and *dule* at the other; the tricky *e* sits in the middle like the fulcrum of a seesaw. If the word is particularly difficult for me, I may add it to my list of personal favorites at the back of my daily planner. If the word ends up there, I try to use it often over the next week or so, each time remembering the visual aid that I have created.

To help challenged spellers gain confidence and competence over their written language, thinking about their writing and their spelling processes enhances their sense of personal power and independence. Particularly for the students who walked away from years of spelling lists and tests with the sense that every word in the language needs to be memorized individually, knowing their own spelling process is a liberating and tremendously pragmatic discovery. Encourage students to think about these questions:

- How do I deal with troublesome words?
- What steps do I take to analyze words with which I struggle?

- What strategies do I draw upon to remember the spelling of those words?
- Where and how do I store and reinforce the correct spelling of troublesome words?

With this knowledge of process comes power.

Helping Students Take Charge of Their Spelling

Good spellers rely upon a host of strategies and resources. As discussed earlier, they move through stages of spelling development that are associated with particular types of strategies. As young children, sounding out words is a primary cue for spelling. Later, visual strategies become important cues to spelling, as students blend the way words sound with the way they look. Still later, meaning-based cues help students understand how words are constructed (as with roots, suffixes, and prefixes), why some words have letters that seemingly make no sense (think about the *p* in *pneumonia* and the *m* in *mnemonics*), and why other words have strange combinations of vowels (like *bureaucracy* and *hors d'oeuvres*).

All too often, challenged spellers are unaware that a variety of strategies exists. Many challenged spellers believe that good spellers are, well, just good spellers. It becomes particularly important that we help challenged spellers think consciously about the types of strategies and resources they already use and become aware of others that are available to them. Helping challenged spellers become acquainted with strategies other spellers use, supporting them as they explore the best ways to use various strategies and resources, and investigating with them the potential pitfalls that accompany external aids like spell checkers will arm them with new power over their written language.

The range of external and internal strategies challenged spellers described were illustrated in Figures 3–2 and 3–3 (Chapter 3). While challenged spellers frequently demonstrate their reliance on sound and, to a lesser degree, on the way words look when written down, sometimes challenged spellers take the easy way out: they just use another word. Probably all spellers substitute words at times. However, when the investment in language is high or a specific word is particularly important to the meaning being conveyed, backup strategies are necessary. Dan, a high school student, tells us, "I usually take a stab at it and keep going and then have my friends check it over and make sure I got the right spelling. I ask my friends, my family; if I have to, I'll transfer to a computer and use spell check just to make sure."

Our students need to understand that all spellers can develop a repertoire of strategies. The more personalized these strategies are, the more effective they become for the individual. We explore with them the range of possibilities in minilessons: rules, patterns, and commonly used generalizations; visualization cues like mnemonics, shape pictures, and associations; auditory cues like rhythms, chants, songs, and cheers; kinesthetic cues like shaping a word in the air, tracing it in the palm of the hand, and feeling the word on a sandy or velvety surface. All of these and more provide the added connection that helps firm up the correct spelling of a word. Beyond introducing a strategy in a minilesson and applying it to a particular word, we ask students to find similar words with which they struggle in their own writing and think about which of the strategies we've discussed will help them remember the word.

In Part 3, we open the window to our classrooms to show how we implement spelling instruction within our various curricula and settings.

How Does Strategic Spelling Instruction Look in Real Secondary Classrooms?

I ask students, "Why didn't you use spell check?" and their earnest reply is, "I did." So I guess the tables have turned and I am left asking myself, "Why didn't I teach them things to watch out for when they are using spell check?"

TRACY

10

Teachers Talk About Spelling and Change

As we studied our classrooms and students, we became increasingly aware of their specific needs regarding spelling. Each of us had taught spelling using traditional methods. As we began looking more closely at the dilemmas our students faced because of their spelling, we sensed that our methods of instruction had to change.

Reflecting, we find our growth as teachers of spelling mirrored our growth as teachers of reading and writing. Each of us had developed classrooms that provided interactive, hands-on learning opportunities for students. Within the context of a workshop environment, we found ways to shape more productive spelling experiences for them. That change involved situating spelling more explicitly within process approach to writing, using minilessons for direct instruction, and providing opportunities for peer response and reflection. Though we use these approaches in workshop settings, they are equally adaptable to traditional classrooms.

Spelling Instruction in a Workshop Environment

Just as we each teach minilessons on writing techniques in a variety of genres, we teach minilessons on spelling (see Figure 10–1). Each minilesson, lasting between five and thirty minutes, focuses on one particular topic, which may be as varied as fixing comma splices, eliminating run-on sentences, examining style or voice, analyzing personal spelling errors, or applying a spelling rule to new words. Spelling instruction in our classrooms is situated in a student-centered, meaningful context. When writers make their work public in the world, they usually make sure that it is error free. First draft writing, which may be riddled with spelling errors, is not public writing—yet. Our goal is to teach students strategies to

- when and why spelling counts
- difficult word analysis
- personal spelling histories
- focused discussions on spelling
- mnemonic devices
- root word study
- successful use of spell checkers
- proofreading strategies
- moving beyond proofreading—what next?
- personal spelling lists
- setting spelling goals
- homophones
- strategies (like have-a-go and chunking words into parts)
- reading one's work with new eyes and ears

Figure 10–1. Sample Minilessons

support self-correction, so when they do make the transition to public writing, they have a host of strategies to use.

In our classrooms students expect that they can make errors in the first draft and not be penalized, as they would be for errors made in a final draft. Audience makes all the difference, which is why we try as often as possible to have students write for authentic audiences. When there is an audience, the quality of the students' work improves—and that includes the quality of their spelling. Fundamental to a process approach is teaching our students the skills to become independent writers. Our goal is to give students the time and tools to make their own corrections. Creating an understanding that writing and spelling are processes becomes critical in our approach to teaching spelling.

To understand how spelling fits into each of our classrooms, it is important to understand the philosophy that governs the environment and interactions that take place there. Though a variety of techniques characterize workshop classrooms (see Figure 10–2), each of our classrooms applies these in unique ways. Our background experiences have helped us create a common vision for instruction, emerging from reflection on our own learning as we have identified those characteristics and strategies that have supported us as readers and writers.

Though there are many differences among our classrooms, student exploration in word study is at the root of our practice. We seek to engage students in word study that helps them see both the logic and the remarkable vitality of the

- choice in reading selections and writing topics
- time to engage in real reading and writing in class
- teacher as facilitator of learning
- conferences to support reading and writing (peer and teacher)
- process-oriented approach to reading and writing, including multiple drafts for polished pieces
- collaboration and peer response
- dynamic classroom to facilitate writing, conferencing, revising, and publishing
- authentic tasks that include reading and writing for real purposes
- skills taught within the context of reading and writing

Figure 10–2. Characteristics of Workshop Classrooms

language. When Tracy realized that she needed to change the approach that she was taking, she encouraged her students to become researchers and observers. She wanted them to search out the knowledge that they needed to improve their own spelling. When we teach students how to observe and analyze their own work, then we begin to foster the development of individuals who are intrinsically motivated.

We also realized we needed to help students look at their spelling processes. We would never send our students out blindly to develop their writing processes. Instead, we structure learning environments that provide students the opportunities and skills they need to develop them. We sought to do the same with their spelling processes. The minilessons that we use in our classrooms provide opportunities to engage our students in understanding and developing their own spelling processes and promote metacognitive awareness, helping students discover how they arrive at the spelling of words. For example, Tracy describes her own spelling process to her students in this way:

> [In first draft writing], I just write. If I come to a word that I am unsure how to spell, I circle it. Next I go back and reread what I have written. When I come back to the words I've circled, I either look the words up or write them a few times to see if I can recognize the correct spelling. Next I have someone else, usually my husband, edit my work. After he reads it, I read it again and I focus on each word. I try to read it as if I have never read it before. Even after I do a spell check, I pay close attention to words that the spell check will let go: words like *their*, *they're*, and *there* are my arch enemies.

We all have a different process when it comes to spelling, and students need guided assistance in developing their own processes.

Two Classrooms from the Inside

Despite the fact that our classrooms reflect common philosophies and beliefs, the scenes that play out in each vary. The stories that follow illustrate the ways individual teachers and their students make time and space for spelling instruction. Karen and Tracy take us into their classrooms to help us see how they contextualize spelling instruction within writing and share with us some day-to-day essential elements of their spelling emphasis.

Teaching Spelling in Karen's Middle School Classroom

Karen doesn't devote lots of time in her middle school classroom to the exclusive teaching of spelling each day, nor does she give weekly spelling tests. She does schedule substantial blocks of time each Tuesday, Wednesday, and Thursday for writing. Since spelling is a writing skill, her direct instruction of spelling occurs within writing minilessons throughout the year.

Although Karen prefers spelling to be taught within the context of student writing, sometimes she focuses just on spelling concepts in order to foster a deeper understanding that she cannot address in a minilesson. For example, Karen's root word study unit addresses spelling in an intensive way. Karen teaches the root word study in the first month of school, emphasizing particular roots over several weeks. The unit serves as a foundation for her to build on throughout the year. The class studies roots such as *act*, *aud*, *cred*, and *luc*. Figure 10–3 is an example of the activities in Karen's class during a focused unit on spelling.

To begin the unit, she explains that knowing how to spell part of a word, like *aud*, can help when spelling other words that include the same root. Root words can also help in understanding the meaning of words. For many students, seeing that words are connected and do not need to be learned entirely independently of each other is a revelation and a relief.

Karen has students find partners and gives each group a root word with its definition. Students spend the next half hour finding words that include their assigned root using dictionaries and other resources. For instance, if their root word is *aud*, they might find words such as *auditorium*, *auditory*, and *audition*. Next, students illustrate the definition of the root word on a poster and include the other example words. For example, students might draw an ear for the root word *aud*. Then, students present their work to the class, in short one- to two-minute presentations. Karen schedules a maximum of three presentations each day so students can have sufficient time to process the information without being overloaded. The word posters are hung around the room for reinforcement, and Karen refers students to the posters throughout the year when they are having difficulty with the spelling, definition, or usage of one of the targeted words. Later,

Monday	Tuesday	Wednesday	Thursday	Friday
Partners work together with root word study (see below).

Students find at least five words that include the root.

Students share their words in small groups. | Review root words.

Teacher conducts minilesson modeling root word illustrations.

Students apply info from minilesson and create their own root word illustrations. | Teacher conducts minilesson on how to present root words.

Students take time to practice their speeches and presentations.

Presentations may begin. | Presentations (3)

Teacher conducts minilesson on developing an awareness of root words in literature.

Read part of the Greek myth "Prometheus."

Students search text for word roots.

Discuss student observations as a large group. | Presentations (3)

Reading time (choice books)

Journal write: Did you notice any root words when you were reading? Did you use roots to help you to understand the meaning of a word?

Share. |

Figure 10–3. Karen's Schedule During Root Word Study

additional words may be added to posters as they come up in reading or discussion.

The intensive unit that Karen teaches on root words is only one example of how she teaches spelling. She believes that the best use of student time and the maximum impact for spelling improvement comes from integrating spelling and writing. The chart shown in Figure 10–4 illustrates the last week of a memoir unit to show how spelling was incorporated within the framework of a larger unit. Though spelling isn't taught in a minilesson every day, it permeates the entire writing atmosphere.

At the beginning of writing days, Karen spends approximately ten minutes reviewing identified writing skills, some of which address particular concerns about spelling. The word study unit described earlier helps build awareness of the richness and interesting qualities of language. Later in the year, spelling minilessons often concentrate on areas where Karen sees many problems, such as homophones. For instance, many of her middle school students have a hard time distinguishing between homophones like *here* and *hear* and *their* and *there*. In focused discussions, Karen helps her students create mnemonic clues for

Monday	Tuesday	Wednesday	Thursday	Friday
Teacher conducts minilesson on how to choose a book for choice reading. Individual reading time Small-group sharing about book	Third draft of memoir is due. Teacher conducts minilesson on "round 'em up" strategy (where students circle words that they question the spelling of). Revising/editing time (Students check their circled words using themselves, word walls, peers, and in-class resources, such as dictionary, thesaurus, computer, and personal spelling lists.)	Teacher conducts minilesson reviewing the grading rubric and how to give constructive responses. Peer conferences Sharing time	Teacher conducts minilesson on how to write a self-reflection letter, showing them a model to explain how to fill out the evaluation rubric. Writing time for students to complete the letter and rubric. Students turn in personal spelling list with their final drafts. Sharing time	Book talk on *Speak*, by Laurie Halse Anderson Reading time Journal write: Who is your favorite character in your book? Why?

Figure 10–4. Spelling Within an Intensive Unit on Memoir Writing

associating troublesome words such as these to support their spelling, like finding *here* in *there* and remembering that we *hear* with our *ear*. Though not new tricks for spelling, they nonetheless provide welcome support to confused middle school students.

Two activities that are ongoing throughout the year are the development of word walls and personal spelling lists. Both strategies, described earlier, provide opportunities for Karen's students to focus on words over time, to reflect on words as they write, and to take ownership for correct spelling in their written work. Word walls in Karen's classroom link to content studies and to high-use words, providing a readily available resource when students use these words in writing. Personal spelling lists give Karen and her students the opportunity to target words that are individually troublesome for students and simultaneously serve as a resource for correct spelling when students write. Parents can help, too, by encouraging students to add problem words to their individual spelling lists.

This type of spelling instruction helps students work on their own words and try new strategies that may help them remember the correct spelling of those words. Because these strategies provide lots of support, they encourage students to take risks with new words. Students don't get marked down for spelling in their early drafts. They have lots of strategies to draw upon for personal editing—like their personal lists of most challenging words—and someone who can check for spelling errors before they turn in their final drafts. If students can find strategies that work for them, they hand in papers without spelling errors.

At the end of each quarter, Karen's students compile a portfolio that includes two of their best pieces of writing over the last weeks, a paper that explains the processes used while writing the pieces, a reflection that discusses what they have improved on and what they still need to work on, a spelling list of words they have misspelled and are still learning, a reading list of books they have completed and journal entries about them, and goals for reading and writing. Spelling is an integral part of the portfolio, not overemphasized or ignored in the collection of what is valued.

Clearly, one important goal in Karen's classroom is to encourage her middle schoolers to write with confidence and independence. By surrounding her students with resources, she makes sure they are constantly immersed in language. The use of a process approach to writing requires that students think about their language as they hone final drafts. Doing so in such a language-rich environment provides repeated exposure to correctly spelled words and reinforces the types of strategies stressed in her minilessons. Students transport their theoretical knowledge immediately into writing they care about and plan to share in a published form.

Teaching Spelling in Tracy's High School Classroom

When Tracy began her September class with, "I have a confession to make," heads perked up from their 8 A.M. slumber. Students eagerly waited to hear a deep, dark confession from their English teacher. Tracy was nervous admitting what would likely make every other English teacher in the department cringe. Standing in front of her students, she squeaked, "I don't know how to spell *no one* and *decide*."

The students looked at her with confusion, then relief as they realized they were not alone in their spelling struggles. Tracy continued, "I avoid using these words if I can't look them up, and no matter how many times I look them up, I can't remember them. For *no one*, I can never remember if it is one word or two separate words. When I try to spell *decide,* I always end up misspelling it like either *deciede* or *deceide*. I need your help in figuring out how I can remember how to spell these words so I never have to look them up again."

Students worked in pairs to devise different ways to remember each of these words. After a few minutes they shared their solutions. One of her students pointed out that if *no one* were one word, it would sound like *noon-e*. He scrunched up his face and drew out the long *e* sound as if he were a coyote howling at the moon. For *decide*, another student came up with "only *I* have to decide" to help her remember she only needs to think about *i* when she spells *decide*.

By sharing two of her own high-frequency spelling demons, Tracy created an environment that encouraged students to take control of some of their own troublesome words. The students already knew some high-use words that gave them trouble, but Tracy knew that there were others that they weren't thinking about.

Tracy had students try to spell one hundred words from the fourth- to eighth-grade spelling placement inventory created by Gentry. For the most part students wrote the words from grades 4 and 5 without moaning; however, at grade 6 the moaning was in full force. Students' faces tensed as they wrote, erased, and rewrote these high-frequency words. Her students' scores ranged from 36 to 89. It became clear that many of her students had substantial gaps in their abilities to spell even these high-use words.

Tracy felt she couldn't plunge forward with high school vocabulary and spelling when students were struggling with fourth- and fifth-grade high-frequency words. She needed an individualized approach that would empower the student who scored 36 just as much as it would the student who scored 89.

Tracy had students pick two words from their test that they were constantly using and misspelling—words that they wanted to know how to spell. Tracy showed students examples of mnemonic devices that former students had made up, which served as models for the students. Students worked in groups developing spelling strategies. In this exercise spelling became very personal. One group made up a mnemonic device for the word *February* because they constantly forgot the first *r*. Students spent a few minutes drawing or creatively writing their selected spelling words and mnemonic devices.

At the end of the hour when everyone joined in a circle to share the words, a dialogue opened up. As one group talked about a word, other students around the room started nodding and writing down the strategy, thanking one another for developing the mnemonic devices. Students hung their words and the pictures or the phrases that helped them around the room for others to see and use. This exercise put the students in charge of their spelling and allowed students time to discuss spelling.

Talking raised student's awareness of spelling. Tracy's conversation with her ninth through twelfth graders revealed that they had never before really talked about spelling. Opening up conversations with students, as simple as it sounds, is one strategy to understand the difficulties students have with spelling and raise their awareness of meaningful strategies. Tracy began class one day by having students respond in their journals to the following four questions:

1. Why do people misspell words?
2. Why do you misspell words?
3. Do you care about spelling? If yes, when?
4. What strategies do you use for spelling?

From these four simple questions, Tracy learned how much spelling affects her students' self-esteem and perceptions of intelligence. Their responses helped launch their discussion of spelling and revealed a consistent sense of helplessness. Tracy was shocked to find how little time her students had actually spent reflecting on spelling in school, particularly in light of the countless hours they had devoted to spelling words correctly for tests. Students listed their spelling strategies: dictionaries, spell checkers, teachers, and parents. Because each of these strategies relies on something beyond the student, Tracy needed to teach her students to take control of their own spelling.

Tracy identified a need to remove herself from the role of editor for her students. Jake helped her understand the dependency that could develop when she held that role. Tracy remembers Jake sitting at a computer, typing his article one word at a time using only his pointer finger. As soon as the slow click, click, click of the keyboard stopped, Jake asked her to look at the article. She started to read it, and when she came to the first error—*were* spelled *where*—she asked him to read it to her, looking at each word and reading only what was on the screen. He quickly read the first line, reading *where* as *were*. She stopped him and asked him to read it again, looking closely at each word. Again he zoomed past the error. Again she asked him to slow down and, pointing to each word, asked him to read them one by one. This time he saw that there was something wrong with the word *where*, but he didn't know what it was. His first strategy was to ask Tracy, "How do you spell this?" Resisting the trap, she asked him to play around with different possible spellings. He eventually came up with the correct spelling on his own.

Jake wanted to know how to spell the word *were* correctly. He merely needed the guidance to find the correct answer on his own, instead of having it given to him. One of the strategies that Tracy used in the conference with him was to have him write the word *were* different ways. It wasn't until his fifth try that he wrote the word correctly, and he could independently recognize that it was correct. Once he learned how to spell *were*, he was able to correct his misspelling of that same word later on in his paper. When given the time and support to really study his work, he could self-correct many words.

Later in this same piece, Jake consistently misused *there* and *their*. Again, Tracy asked him to explain the difference between the two words to her. He told her that *there* was a place and that *their* showed possession. She asked him to go back and circle every *there* and *their* in his piece, helping Jake apply what he was learning immediately to his own writing. Next she asked him to check each *there* and *their* to make sure that he had the right one in the right place. This time, he was able to go back and self-correct his work.

The corrections that Jake made with *there* and *their* were a result of applying information to his writing that he already knew. When Tracy asked him what each of the words meant, he knew their meanings, yet in his story he wrote "*there* shoes." When Tracy asked him why he used the word *there* in that context, he was able to recognize his mistake and self-correct it. Jake didn't know how to proof-read his work and apply his knowledge of homophones to his writing. He needed to practice applying the information to his writing and making the corrections himself instead of strengthening his dependency on other people to make the corrections. It was time for Jake to take responsibility for his spelling.

If Jake hadn't known the difference between *their* and *there*, Tracy's role would have been to teach him the difference. However, since he knew the difference between them, her role as a teacher changed to encouraging him and insisting that he apply the information. In this case, Tracy needed to understand clearly what Jake needed from her. He was asking for the correct spelling, but what he needed was the guidance and encouragement to prove to himself that he could self-correct his work. Tracy works hard to engage her students in conversations and personal study of spelling so that they can take control over words that have been out of their control for too long.

Tracy's Journalism Class: Spelling for Extended Audiences

Students get involved with spelling in Tracy's journalism class, where they produce a twelve-page newspaper every other week:

> The computer lab was full of students by the time I got down there—a few minutes before class officially began. Students were already at computers and working on their pages. It was production day, which meant that we stayed until we sent the paper out. The computer lab always hovers around eighty degrees, but on production days it seems more like ninety because of the energy and movement in the room. On one such day, Adam sat staring at his computer; he was trying to master a perfectly laid out page. His copy editing team had worked to correct the articles from his page. He was handed an article and asked to make the changes. He asked, "Why didn't they [the authors] do a spell check? Why are there all of these errors?"

Unlike a typical writing class where students produce writing for a small audience, students in journalism classes produce writing for hundreds to thousands of outside readers. Audience affects the students' writing and editing process. Students in Tracy's class sit huddled together in small groups of three and four. They pass pages of the paper around the circle until everyone has read every article. Their heads are burrowed down so Tracy sees only the tops of them as they intensely read their peers' work. Occasionally a student will interrupt a member of his group and ask them a question about spelling or grammar.

Students end up in grammar and spelling conversations and debate which form of *there* to use, whether *its* has an apostrophe, and when they should use a comma. The minilessons for future classes stem from issues that emerge from page editing during the production session. Minilessons always come from students' needs (see Figure 10–5). Common student needs include learning the distinction between particularly troublesome homophones like *there/their*, *it's/its*, *where/were*, and *are/our* and practicing self-correction techniques such as round 'em up and have-a-go. Using a round 'em up strategy, students search a paper—or in this case an entire newspaper page—to find the same type of error that has previously been identified. In other classrooms, students may search for those words that are frequently misspelled in the paper. Often, clearing up one such error makes a noticeable difference in the paper. With the have-a-go strategy, students write a word multiple times, searching for the most accurate-looking way of spelling it.

- raise awareness of possible strategies
- personalize mnemonics for troublesome words
- round up errors (after correcting an error, look for all the other examples in the same paper and correct them as well)
- conference with peers or teacher
- have-a-go (writing a word multiple times to determine the most likely correct spelling)
- build ownership through writing for real audiences and for real purposes
- raise awareness of possible strategies
- personalize mnemonics for troublesome words
- round up errors (after correcting an error, look for all the other examples in the same paper and correct them as well)
- conferences with peers or teacher
- have-a-go (writing a word multiple times to determine the most likely correct spelling)
- build ownership through writing for real audiences and for real purposes

Figure 10–5. Tracy's Strategies

Computer-savvy students report typing words multiple ways and looking for the red line that accompanies misspellings. Generally, after one or two attempts, they are able to arrive at a correct spelling.

In a production-oriented class like journalism, students use each other for resources and safety nets when it comes to spelling errors, just as Tracy uses her husband. These students care about each other's work because they know that each piece of the student newspaper reflects on all of them.

After five hours of page and copy editing, Tracy's students still fear finding yet another error buried in an article. They feel they could copyedit forever and there would still be changes. In this production-oriented class, there is a clear audience for whom they are writing and clear reasons that they are copyediting. In Tracy's regular writing class, the reasons aren't as clear. Giving a paper to her is neither the same as having it sent all over the country nor same as having peers at school read it.

In our classrooms we constantly strive to help our students know that the reason to write is to get their voices heard. Our students need to know that their words and opinions matter to their peers, parents, teachers, and community. So often, their words are muddled by misspellings that misconstrue their message to their public. It is our job to help them find ways to make their powerful voices heard clearly. For too long, we have relied on texts that, of necessity, espouse a one-size-fits-all approach. Instead, we need to base our instruction on professional judgment supported by our own careful observation of our students and their work. As teachers, it is important to know a variety of strategies that support student growth in spelling. Then, after looking closely at the types of needs our students demonstrate, we can make decisions about which types of strategies might make the most difference in our students' spelling expertise. As Karen reminds us, "Each classroom, each teacher, and each student is different; we must trust ourselves and our students to find and use the strategies that work well in our own classrooms."

11

Approaches to Teaching Spelling

*As I begin the new school year, I contemplate the role that spelling
has in my classroom. It's strange that at the beginning of my
teaching career, spelling consumed over half of my class time.
Now, after weeding it out of my classroom for over three years, I
realize that it's time to bring it back.*

—Tracy

So, what does all this spelling instruction look like when it's couched in the classroom between teaching novels, running book groups, writing persuasive essays,
disciplining students, and trying to take attendance? Although we spend a small
proportion of our instructional time teaching spelling, our emphasis on spelling is
integral in all of our classrooms. Karen gives this glimpse of her spelling instruction during the first days of school:

> The beginning of the year is set aside to get to know my students, establishing
> workshop routines and creating a sense of community. Within the first month
> of school, I like to begin at least discussing spelling and letting students know
> that spelling is important because it allows writers to communicate with their
> audience. My students are directly out of elementary school and feel instant
> relief when I explain their spelling tests are over with, at least while in my
> classroom.

For all of us, handwritten spelling or literacy autobiographies provide baseline
information at the beginning of the school year. Students write about their experiences with writing and spelling and how they've been taught spelling from the time
of their earliest memories (see Figure 11–1). We think it is important for students
to detail where they have had troubles with spelling and how it has impacted their
view of themselves as spellers and as writers in general. We are aware, as was illustrated in Chapter 10, that poor spelling can translate to a sense of incompetence as
a writer. Not only do these papers give us insight into the histories, attitudes, and
experiences students have regarding spelling, but challenged spellers will make

- Collect first draft student spelling or literacy autobiographies.
- Identify errors on first draft papers.
- Look for categories of errors.
- Engage students in looking for categories of errors.
- Help students think about similarities in the words they've misspelled.
- Set up personal spelling logs and dictionaries.
- Plan minilessons for the term based on student-demonstrated need and the core understandings we want to emphasize.

Figure 11–1. Planning the Spelling Year

themselves known immediately, sometimes through their hesitancy with word use and often by self-identification. From this point, we begin to chart our instructional course for the semester or year. Spelling instruction should be planned for the students who are currently in our classrooms, addressing the needs found in their writing. Otherwise, the lessons we teach may not be relevant to them and may fail to address the real problems they face.

We follow this literacy autobiography with a spelling placement inventory. Jennifer tells her students, "This grade won't count against you; just do your best. This will help us decide the types of word study we need to focus on this year." Students smile and laugh as they cruise through the first lists, spelling words like *me* and *do* with ease. Soon, however, they furrow their brows as the upper levels of the test pose harder words, like *yacht, committee, pursue,* and *restaurant*.

Many students have never thought about the fact that their errors tend to have common features, and finding this out sparks a sense of power and control over their learning and their spelling. Many students just say "I can't spell" for years without actually looking closely at the errors they make. For them, their spelling errors have only been words marked incorrect on the Friday test or in their written work. The placement tests help students begin to identify areas where they need to improve in spelling, helping them become more open to the tools we are able to give them. Jennifer has students write the words they missed on the placement inventory on a separate sheet of paper, not to make them learn the words at this point, but to have them look for similarities in the errors they have made.

The information gleaned from the analysis of first draft writing and the spelling placement inventory provides baseline data for us to begin planning spelling minilessons. Minilessons may be didactic or may simply open up conversations about spelling that lead to word awareness. Though the frequency of the minilessons vary by teacher and grade level, each lesson targets specific information that addresses needs identified from student products.

- memorization
- chunking words in syllables
- have-a-go
- personal dictionaries
- frequently misspelled word lists
- personal spelling logs
- use of editors
- mnemonics
- use of dictionaries and other print resources
- visually based strategies, like shape pictures and tracing words
- technology-supported strategies, like Franklin spellers and spell checkers
- looking for parts of little words in bigger words
- meaning-based strategies, like prefixes, suffixes, and roots
- rule-based strategies like *i* before *e* except after *c*

Figure 11–2. Strategies to Support Spelling

Prior to adopting this strategic approach, our more traditional lessons derived from a spelling book: Students did the lessons that stretched across the week, they took pre- and posttests, they received answers and a score, and they moved on. Within that context, spelling was seldom talked about as a meaningful and interesting part of language study. Important questions were never considered: What does spelling mean to students? Where does their frustration with spelling lie? What do they fear most about spelling?

Through our classroom conversations about spelling, we are able to softly share a wealth of information that students have the opportunity to immediately apply in their writing (see Figure 11–2). Sometimes we simply explore aspects of spelling process with our students. For example, Karen spends about half an hour of one fifty-minute class period investigating with students the ways they spell a word they don't know. Collaboratively, students brainstorm an amazing repertoire of strategies that are placed on a list and posted on the classroom wall for all to refer to. This list is left up all year and added to as new strategies are identified. Karen notes, "My best spellers have an abundance of spelling strategies and like to model them in front of the class." Strategies from the list are perfect topics for strategy-based minilessons and help all students become aware of the strategies that good spellers take for granted.

In addition to student-identified strategies, we want to help all students explore new strategies and gain new knowledge that will help them push their own competencies as spellers and writers. As described in Part 2, What Do

Challenged Spellers Need?, we seek to address each of the core understandings (see Figure 6–1) in an ongoing fashion throughout the semester or school year.

If students are turned off by spelling, we engage in lots of strategies that encourage play with language—human words, mnemonic devices, shape drawings, scavenger hunts to find particular types of words or words that fit specific patterns or rules, literature circle discussions about cool vocabulary words, and competitive word searches for word walls.

If students fail to recognize that rules or patterns generalize to entire groups of words, we focus on strategies that help them see logic in the language, including learning rules (see Figure 8–3); studying prefixes, suffixes, and roots through webs, word walls, and word analysis (breaking really intriguing words into parts to discover their meanings); and doing word sorts.

If students tend to misspell words that are exceptionally high use, we open up conversations about the fact that a relatively few words make up most of the words we use in everyday writing (see Figures 9–1 and 9–2), and we emphasize strategies to support remembering those words. These strategies include keeping personal spelling lists, creating homophone card sets, making use of frequently misspelled word lists, building word walls, and creating personal cues or mnemonics to help them remember correct spellings. If students don't understand how or when to use resources, we work with collaborative projects like the brainstormed list of strategies described earlier. We also talk about the appropriate use of editors, spell checkers, and other resources. In some cases, we teach students in a straightforward manner how to use a dictionary, conference on a paper, or work with an editor.

Use of any of these approaches is based on one critical factor: each must meet an observed student need. Thus we come full circle. First we set about finding out what our students know and what they need to know about spelling. Then we plan our program, based on student need. Though instruction certainly has similarities from year to year, it is also true that no two years, or even semesters, are exactly alike.

Organizing for Instruction

It is true that spelling, for all of us, is taught in small increments and within the structure of a workshop classroom. Spelling is most often taught through whole-class minilessons. When we see evidence that information has not transferred to student writing, we begin to plan individual and small-group conferences for reinforcement. For example, when Jennifer's students are learning about homophones, the lesson is directed to the entire group. Students take out their one-inch binder rings and add the new punched index cards containing the set of homophones being taught. Jennifer discusses the sets and gives examples for the students to add to their cards before placing the cards back into their binders. If a particular student, or group of students, continues to struggle with a set of words—say, *quit*, *quite*, and *quiet*—she will begin individual or small-group conferences as appropriate. Even though these are not homophones per se, Jennifer has found these cards to be a very effective tool for helping students remember the correct spelling and use for each word.

Not all of the instruction is geared toward all students. At times it is important to deal with students one-on-one or in small groups to discuss spelling issues. By addressing spelling issues in whole-class, small-group, and individual settings, we are reinforcing what we've already taught. Even if a rule has been presented in a whole-class setting, many students may need to hear and see the information several times before it becomes a part of their knowledge base that can be comfortably applied to actual writing.

On a typical day, several activities might be going on at the same time. After a minilesson, students begin writing on topics they have chosen; a low hum is often heard around the room as students share work or discuss topics with one another. When they are immersed in their own writing, that is the time when we, as teachers, find time and space for conferencing. Conferencing is an important part of a workshop classroom and offers tremendous instructional benefit. It is through conferencing that the teacher can address individual writing or reading problems with students on a one-on-one basis, differentiating instruction as needed. These individual conferencing moments provide rich opportunities to reinforce spelling strategies and address unique spelling needs.

Students are generally selected for conferences when Jennifer is perusing rough drafts. Once a teacher is committed to improving spelling in the classroom, it is not difficult to identify those who have the greatest problems. Error analysis information gathered in the beginning weeks of school also helps both the teacher and the students become aware of personal spelling issues that may be addressed during a conference.

As the spelling conference begins, Jennifer asks what the student is working on and how the particular piece is going. After discussing the progress on the work, Jennifer directs the discussion to a particular spelling issue. With Andy, the focus of one conference was whether to double a consonant when adding a suffix beginning with a vowel, a common spelling issue in eighth grade.

JENNIFER: Andy, I notice you are having difficulty with some types of words over and over. For instance, I see that you often double consonants in words when you're not supposed to and actually change the meaning of what you're writing. Look here—you've written "Marjorie was *starring* into the night sky," as the lead to your story. I think you mean *staring*.

ANDY: Yeah, that's what I wanted to say.

JENNIFER: Remember, *stare* is a silent *e* word and *-ing* is a suffix that begins with a vowel. So, according to the rule, how would we deal with adding this *-ing* ending?

Jennifer reviewed the rule with him once again and pointed out the poster on the word wall, where he could have immediate visual access to the rule instead of having to look it up in the spelling section of his binder.

JENNIFER: Do you remember the silent *e* rule we learned last week?

ANDY: [*Looking at the poster*] Well . . . since we don't hear the *e* and the suffix starts with *i*, you must not double the final *r*.

JENNIFER: Okay, let's try another word. How about *share*? Can you write this and use the rule? Then, I want you to tell me the rule that you used. . . .

Jennifer asked Andy to be aware when he was writing other silent *e* words that needed suffixes and to put a check in the margin near them so when he turned the paper in she could see that he was consciously using the rule as he wrote.

It is possible to conference with a group of students about spelling in much the same way. Four or five students with the same consistent spelling issue are gathered in a single spot. These conferences begin with a short, focused minilesson drawing the students' attention to a particular rule or skill and often referencing posters or word walls in the classroom. For example, if students are having difficulty remembering exceptions to the *i* before *e* except after *c* rule, they might discuss words like *their* and *weird*. Jennifer sees errors with these words consistently. This is not surprising; after all, the words don't follow the pattern set forth in the rule. She usually suggests that the students work together for a few minutes to come up with a mnemonic device to use for remembering these exceptions. One group of students worked together and came up with the following sentence:

Their confusion about the exceptions to the *i* before *e* except after *c* rule was *weird* to *their* teacher.

All of the students in the small group wrote their sentence somewhere in their binder so they could find it easily. Thus, they produced a mnemonic device for remembering the most common exceptions to the rule and spelling instruction was once again individualized.

Whether the teacher is working with an individual or a small group, these miniconferences take only about five to seven minutes each, and oftentimes less, making it possible to have conferences with many individuals or small groups in one class period. In the longer stretch of writing time afforded in a block schedule, it is possible to meet with all students in a single class session.

Finding Time

We do not teach a spelling minilesson every day of the week, though a week never goes by when spelling is not addressed. Jennifer generally schedules at least one minilesson each week and plans some sort of reinforcement of that minilesson during the rest of the week. When it comes time for a final draft to be turned in, those spelling lessons appear, in some form, on the writing rubric.

On a Tuesday morning, thirty students shuffle into Jennifer's classroom and have to be reminded to copy their homework from the board. Students will have ninety minutes of time in Jennifer's classroom and, on this particular day, the entire block is devoted to writing. Jennifer circles the room to be sure each student has written his or her homework in his or her planner, and then she instructs students to open their binders to the spelling section. Students are learning the rule about when to drop *y* to add *i* when making a word plural. So far during the school year, Jennifer has detected many *frys* and *crys* in writing instead of *fries* and *cries*.

The rule, which has been typed up in large letters with examples, is distributed to each student. Jennifer has found over the years of teaching spelling in this format that if she has students copy the rule and example from the overhead, two things will invariably happen. First, some students will not copy the examples properly, which in the long run doesn't help them if they want to use the notes as a reference. Second, students will copy at such differing paces that some won't hear a word of explanation because they are still laboriously trying to get the words transcribed from overhead to lined paper.

So Jennifer gives each student a copy of the rule sheet and displays the same sheet on the overhead. As Jennifer reviews the rule, she asks students to make notes in the margins to keep their attention focused. She asks them:

> What other examples can you think of that reflect this rule or pattern?
> In the future, how will you know if the word is spelled incorrectly?
> Of the words that fit this rule but nonetheless give you trouble, how will you remember them in the future?

Jennifer asks students to read words like *frys* and *crys* singly and to pronounce them aloud. "'Fris' and 'cris,'" come the giggly responses. She then points out to the students that when they see words alone without the context of a sentence, it's often easier to see that they don't look correct. She then reminds them to try have-a-go as another option for finding the correct spelling of a word.

Jennifer points out that with a suffix beginning with a vowel, such as *-ing*, they must keep the *y* of the original word. Again, she asks them to look at the word and its spelling. If they changed the *y* to *i* in this instance, they would see *friing* and *criing*. "Would you know those words were incorrect if you saw them spelled that way?" she asks. Heads bob in response. At the end of the minilesson Jennifer asks students to keep the rule on their desks until the end of the block time, just in case they need to refer to it again. Jennifer asks them to do this as a semiconstant reminder of their new learning for the day. Students now continue writing until it is time for a five-minute break, after which they are introduced to another minilesson on writing.

Their writing minilesson addresses some aspect of the craft of writing, such as adding detail, writing a good lead, or shrinking time to move ahead in a piece. Students keep notes for these minilessons in their language arts notebooks. They then have another stretch of writing time, during which they can practice the skills they learned over the course of the block. At the end of the block, when students are packing up to leave, Jennifer reminds them to file the spelling rule sheet in their binders.

Minilessons for focused instruction fit just as well in traditional classrooms. Teachers can begin class with a focused five- to seven-minute look at an aspect of spelling. This brings the class together and allows them to focus on a skill they will use later in the day or week. It is important that these lessons be related to errors students make or to new information they will be applying in their writing. If the spelling lessons aren't relevant to the students' work at hand, or cannot be generalized to a broad spectrum of words, students will see them as insignificant and removed from the learning in the classroom, just as they did the weekly spelling lessons from a textbook. Sometimes it helps to see an actual layout of an instructional block to clarify how a curricular focus takes shape. Jennifer's block looks something like the weeklong plan shown in Figure 11–3.

It is important to teach and reteach spelling skills and to cover a small area of language study deeply. When information comes too fast or in too shallow a fashion, students often express frustration and hopelessness. Instead, through repeated minilessons, students are exposed to very focused spelling skills that can be generalized to a wide arena of words. If students know the spelling rule or skill well, they will be more likely to use it and generalize it to the appropriate words.

Sometimes the instructional setting is shaped by thematic or genre units or the reading of whole-class novels. For example, Jennifer teaches a multiweek thematic study titled *Affluenza*, based on a concept from a PBS documentary that describes overconsumption by the American public as a disease. During the unit, students view the videotape *Affluenza*, which can be obtained through most local libraries, do writings about various aspects of the topic, work in small groups to engage in introspective discussions, and look at advertising. The study ends with

Monday

minilesson: spelling rule: silent *e* words (5–7 minutes)
talk about topic selection for next paper (5 minutes)
status of the class (2 minutes)
writing time (25 minutes)—teacher writing and spelling conferences
group share (5 minutes)

Tuesday

minilesson: using active verbs in writing (5–7 minutes)
status of the class (2 minutes)
writing time (30 minutes)—teacher writing and spelling conferences
group share (5 minutes)

Wednesday

minilesson: using KWL when you read (10 minutes)
reading workshop (30 minutes)—teacher writing and spelling conferences
group share (5 minutes)

Thursday

minilesson: adding detail to your writing (5–7 minutes)
status of the class (2 minutes)
writing time (30 minutes)—teacher writing and spelling conferences
group share (5 minutes)

Friday

minilesson: analyzing the lead of your novel (10 minutes)
reading workshop (30 minutes)—teacher does reading record*
best book share (5 minutes)

*Reading record provides the teacher an opportunity to quickly record students' reading progress.

Figure 11–3. Workshop Classroom (45-Minute Period)

a field trip to the local mall, where they continue looking at ways advertising targets them for overconsumption.

The unit begins with a look at the word *affluenza* and its base, so the unit is grounded in a discussion of roots and language.

> Today we're going to begin looking at some of our habits we have when it comes to shopping and how you, as teenagers, are targeted by advertising companies into thinking you never have enough. You are always supposed to want more, and we consume many times the amount of goods that people did in the 1950s. The name given to this "disease," as it's referred to in the video, is affluenza. So, let's start out by looking at the root of the word. What word do you see in *affluenza*? How could that relate to what we're going to talk about?

Some students invariably come up with the word *affluence* and define it for the class. Discussion builds around questions about what *affluence* is and how affluent the surrounding area might be.

On Monday students watch a portion of the video and then take a fun quiz on some facts about consumption in the present day. All units, regardless of topic, feature minilessons or activities that target previously identified areas of spelling concern. This week students are asked to add a homonym card for *there*, *their*, and *they're* to their homonym rings and discuss why it is important to know the differences among these words. Thereafter, they have examples and definitions on the card to use as a reference.

The following week, students begin discussing advertising and how many techniques in advertising are aimed at teenagers because they have disposable income and are easily persuaded that they need something. The focus in spelling for the week is one of the spelling rules, which they add to their binders. The connection for the discussion, however, is the importance of spelling in advertising. The class discusses the following questions: Why would it be important for copywriters to spell correctly? When is it okay for an advertiser to misspell a word? What happens when a sign or advertisement in a magazine has a word misspelled? Students talk about credibility and clarity following the rule for the week. Later, when students write their own "subvertisements," they are quite critical with each other when words are misspelled in the ads. An awareness has been planted of the importance of spelling in a real context.

Evaluating Spelling

An important question in most minds is, How do we evaluate spelling if we aren't using lists and tests anymore? Do we simply add a separate grade for spelling in final draft rubrics? Do we ignore it when we correct drafts after spending considerable instructional time on it? What is the appropriate level of response for those who have been instructed and still turn in work with frequent spelling errors? In each of our classrooms, we have agreed that spelling doesn't become an issue until a final or best draft is turned in. Until then, we can instruct through minilessons, practice with students, conference with them about the spelling in their writing, but we don't penalize students. If spelling interferes with understanding in an early draft, we ask the student to work on the draft to make it clear.

Students may be attentive and take serious notes during spelling minilessons. Ears perk up, and they nod in agreement during spelling conferences. They really seem to understand the spelling skills being taught and make a considerable effort at self-correction in rough draft writing, as evidenced by cross-outs and multiple attempts to spell many words. And then, final drafts come in, riddled with homonym errors and words they could have corrected if they had only proofread or gone back into their spelling notes before turning the papers in. The question is, How much do we respond to these students? Should we red circle their rough drafts in order to catch their attention before it's too late? As noted earlier, in our classes, we don't penalize students for incorrect spelling on rough drafts, journals, or literature responses. We want to know what the students have to say and how they have gone about saying it before we deal with errors.

When it comes to final drafts, we all agree that correct spelling is important. The spelling logs found in Appendixes D and E contain a section where the student or teacher writes down misspelled words, which then go into the spelling log in the student's binder. We ask the students to think about why the word or words were misspelled or overlooked in proofreading. It is through this process that students must think about mistakes and will likely transfer correct spellings to long-term memory.

Even in final papers, though spelling does count, it does so in relation to other major considerations—like organization, fluency, content, word choice, and style. Within that framework, mechanics, while still important, are not raised to unrealistic proportions in the final grade. Though the weight we place on spelling in final draft writing is ultimately an individual decision, the rubric shown in Figure 11–4 and Appendix G offers some insight into how one teacher evaluates spelling within the context of writing.

Rubrics give students clear information about what we value as teachers and how their work will be graded. Clearly, rubrics are personal and must reflect the needs of the teacher and the subject matter of the class. However, regardless of the application, rubrics can help us to keep clear in our own minds the qualities we are looking for in our students' writing. As you see, mechanics is one of six major writing traits this teacher values. And, within the trait labeled "mechanics," only one of the considerations is spelling. Within this framework, spelling is important but not disproportionate to the overall quality of the piece.

Ideas and Content	Organization	Conventions
5 This paper is clear, focused, and interesting. It holds the reader's attention. Relevant details enrich the central theme or story line.	5 The organization enhances and showcases the central idea or theme. The order, structure, or presentation is compelling and moves the reader through the text.	5 The writer shows a good grasp of standard writing conventions (e.g., grammar, capitalization, punctuation, usage, spelling, paragraphing) and uses them effectively.
3 This paper is clear and focused, even though the overall result may not be captivating. Support is attempted, but it may be limited.	3 The reader can readily follow what's being said, but the overall organization may sometimes be ineffective or too obvious.	3 Errors, while not overwhelming, begin to impair readability. While errors do not block meaning, they tend to be distracting.
1 This paper lacks a central idea or purpose or forces the reader to make inferences based on very sketchy details.	1 Organization is haphazard and disjointed. The writing lacks direction. Ideas, details, or events are loosely strung together.	1 Many errors in conventions distract the reader and make the text difficult to read.

Word Choice	Sentence Fluency	Voice
5 Words convey the intended message in an interesting, precise, and natural way. The writing is full and rich yet concise.	5 The writing has an easy flow and rhythm when read aloud. Sentences are well built with consistently strong and varied structures.	5 The writer speaks directly to the reader in a way that is individualistic, expressive, and engaging. Clearly, the writer is involved in the text and intends the writing to be read.
3 The language, though ordinary, conveys the message; though functional, it may lack excitement or "punch," resulting in a paper without flair.	3 Sentences tend to be mechanical rather than fluid. The text hums along efficiently for the most part.	3 The writer seems sincere but not fully involved in the topic. The result is pleasant, acceptable, sometimes even personal, but not compelling.
1 The writer struggles with a limited vocabulary, groping for words to convey meaning. Often the language is vague and abstract or redundant and devoid of details.	1 The paper is difficult to follow or to read aloud. Sentences tend to be choppy, incomplete, rambling, irregular, or just very awkward.	1 The writer seems wholly indifferent, uninvolved, or dispassionate. The writing is flat, lifeless, stiff, or mechanical.

Rubric modeled after the Northwest Lab's Six-Trait Assessment of Writing

Figure 11–4. Writing Rubric

5 Student spells emphasized high-frequency words correctly throughout the final draft paper and uses resources (spell check, dictionaries, charts in class) and/or editors to correctly spell most words—including words specific to the topic.

3 Student spells correctly most high-frequency words in the final draft paper. Misspellings of other words, though apparent, do not interfere with the ability to read and comprehend the message of the paper.

1 Student misspells many high-frequency words and does not appear to draw upon resources to support spelling of other words. Misspellings make it difficult to read and comprehend the paper.

© 2003 by Rebecca Bowers Sipe from *They Still Can't Spell?* Portsmouth, NH: Heinemann.

Figure 11–5. Spelling Rubric

It may be helpful to think about a rubric for spelling, if that is a goal we are emphasizing (see Figure 11–5). The teacher using this rubric clearly wants her students to focus on the words and strategies that have been emphasized: in this case, high-frequency words and strategies such as use of editors, wall charts, dictionaries, and spell checks. Because spelling is just one of the six traits for assessing a paper, challenged spellers are not overpenalized for their area of weakness. At the same time, spelling receives emphasis, and thereby, the tools and strategies we are striving to teach our students do, too. Rubrics create a win-win situation, especially when they are reinforced consistently across the curriculum.

It's important to note that in some of our classes, spelling is not considered as a reason to lower grades. If there are spelling errors, the corrections are addressed in the student's spelling log. If a paper has more spelling errors than the teacher finds acceptable, the student may be asked to turn in another draft, one that has been proofread with a peer coach's or teacher's assistance. We must remember that some struggling spellers are at a loss even with the use of a spell checker. It isn't penalties they need; it's help and support.

How Do You Take Spelling Change
to the Home Front?

Most of us don't resist change, we resist being changed.

ANONYMOUS TEACHER AT AN NCTE WORKSHOP

12

Implementing Spelling Instructional Change That Lasts

You have to remember, Ann Arbor has a very short attention span . . .

—Ann Arbor teacher

Implementing curricular change involves hard work and risk taking. By definition, changing means moving into unknown territory, doing things differently, making mistakes, experiencing false starts, and even needing to regroup and begin the process all over again.

Openness to change relates not only to us but to our students and their parents, our colleagues, and our administrators as well. In curricular areas like spelling, background experiences affect receptivity and willingness to doing things differently. Challenged spellers in particular may express resistance and loathing when we suggest revisiting an area that has been so unsuccessful for them in the past.

We all want students to leave school with better control over their written language. So, we find ourselves confronting several crucial questions.

- As a teacher at the secondary level, what can I reasonably do to begin to meet the spelling needs of my students?
- As a member of an English department, what steps can I take to help initiate a more thoughtful and effective approach to spelling within the department and across the school as a whole?
- As a teacher or administrator within a district, what can I do to promote a sensible and successful approach to spelling that can be supported district-wide at the secondary level?

Change often comes amid a flurry of activity and support; unfortunately, as observed by the Ann Arbor teacher quoted above, that initial burst of energy and enthusiasm may dwindle within a fairly short time frame unless we've carefully planned a few critical elements. Because we have been involved in supporting spelling change, we will share specific suggestions we've found important to successful curricular change.

Planning for Successful Instructional Change

As we begin to deconstruct changes that work, we find some elements that surface repeatedly, like relevance, knowledge, communication, commitment, support, and time. As we begin to think about changing our approach to spelling in our classrooms, we need to think about each of these in relation to the changes we are considering if we want our changes to be effective and lasting.

Relevance

For instructional changes to be worth our time and effort, they must relate directly to the needs of our students. We've all overheard adults lament the poor spelling of young adults today. These lamentations may sound the alarm, but they seldom tell us anything we don't already know or help us address issues related to spelling. Making changes in the approach to spelling instruction at any level—classroom, department, school, or district—requires a clear understanding of what we are trying to correct.

As discussed earlier, a close look at spelling in actual student writing narrows the scope of issues to consider. On a classroom level, teachers may need only look at a few samples of first draft writing and make a list of the prevalent errors found. If a broader scale of change is being contemplated, perhaps a change in the department's or school's approach to spelling instruction, collecting samples of student first draft writing from a number of teachers and potentially from teachers in a variety of content areas will make it possible to identify error patterns found in many students' work (see Figure 12–1). At Chelsea High School, in Michigan, for example, faculty decided to focus on improvement of writing across the curriculum as one of their North Central Accreditation goals. As a part of this process, students completed a schoolwide writing assessment. These papers provided excellent samples of first draft writing that could be analyzed to identify patterns of spelling errors students tended to make. Papers generated for state-mandated testing often provide other samples of first draft writing that can be copied and used for school-based initiatives. Analysis and discussion of these papers provides a platform for setting goals and beginning curriculum change.

In schoolwide writing assessments, teachers often observe that spelling isn't as bad as might first be believed. Because certain types of words tend to be misspelled repeatedly and particular categories of errors may be problematic throughout a paper or set of papers, they sometimes give the mistaken impression of greater concerns than actually exist. When teachers look at errors across multiple classes, they are apt to find, as we have, that homophones are major culprits. Frequently, students have difficulty with some high-frequency words, because of either faulty sound-letter connections or pronunciation problems. Particularly, challenged spellers tend to exhibit lack of knowledge of spelling rules or generalizations, sometimes incorrectly applying the information they do have.

Whatever categories of errors are found, listing them helps clarify the problems you are trying to solve, moving from "none of these kids can spell" to a less overwhelming position in which faculty acknowledge that students actually have mastered many features of writing and tend to struggle with only specific types of problems.

- Secure sample first draft student papers, preferably from across the department or school.
- Review papers to determine the types of errors students make.
- Talk with other teachers to identify the two or three most prevalent and important types of errors students tend to make.
- Establish a classroom, departmental, or school-wide goal for addressing those errors.

Figure 12–1. Getting Change Started

Once error types are identified, they can become the focus of initial attention. Too often change is derailed because we try to take on everything at once. Remember the student complaint about "too much, too fast, too shallow"? Manageable curricular change tends to focus on important issues first and for a long enough period of time so that students can absorb new information and apply it in their writing. This doesn't mean we, as teachers, will forget the other errors; it means that they will be addressed later or will be dealt with on a one-on-one basis for now.

Think of how powerful it would be to discuss student first draft writing with other teachers, working together to identify the most pressing spelling needs found in *actual* papers. This process of analysis and discussion guarantees the relevance of any spelling-related change effort, establishing the importance of the curricular change in a very immediate and personal way.

Building Knowledge

Once we understand our students' spelling problems and decide where to focus our energies, it is important to look for professional readings that will help inform local and districtwide conversations about spelling in which successful practices are shared and potential courses of action deliberated (see Figure 12–2). In

- Identify materials to read and share. You may wish to have each teacher read a particular piece or have everyone read the same materials.
- Ask for faculty meeting time and support for focused discussions on the readings.
- Interview challenged spellers to learn more about their spelling backgrounds and the strategies they use.
- Talk with colleagues to identify successful practices.
- Build a collection of successful strategies to share.
- Create minilessons (short, focused lessons) that present strategies that address needs you observe in student writing.

Figure 12–2. Building Knowledge

particular, researchers Richard Gentry, Shane Templeton, Diane Snowball, and Donald Bear offer excellent guidance. See Appendix L for an annotated bibliography of knowledge-building materials.

The importance of understanding challenged spellers cannot be stressed enough. If these students are to move forward as spellers, they must have practices to draw upon, practices that support *their* learning and can replace practices that have proven ineffective or even harmful for them. If we continue to meet identified student spelling needs with additional rounds of word lists, exercises, and tests, we are behaving like the doctor who prescribes two more weeks of green pills for the patient who hasn't responded to the first round of green pills. We are unlikely to see any improvement in either attitude or competence regarding spelling.

In addition to understanding challenged spellers, however, we need to identify and share strategies that work. Strategies that we and our colleagues use ourselves and ones that we have used successfully with students provide resources to help a struggling speller when nothing else seems to work.

Communication

Our hectic pace, rushing around taking care of the hundreds of details of our daily jobs, allows little time for us to communicate with our constituencies. First and foremost, of course, are our students. For older students to become invested in new practices, they need to understand what is being changed, why the change is needed, and how they will benefit from it. We spend time in our classrooms talking about the importance of spelling and helping students understand that different levels of spelling expertise are represented among the group. We try to help students fully understand our belief that written communication is crucial to their success now and in the future. Through this communication, we have witnessed a stronger sense of buy-in and motivation.

Students are only one of the groups with whom we communicate. Parents are excited when we talk with or write to them about our interest in spelling improvement. Frequently, school boards are responding to parental concerns when they require weekly lists or districtwide spelling competency tests. In the absence of other strategies, they sometimes respond to external pressures with what they know—more green pills. Newsletters, website postings, classroom telephone hot lines, parent conferences, and class meetings with parents have all been effective in keeping parents informed of the types of changes we are making and why we've decided to make them.

Clearly, a spelling program will have more impact with collaboration across the department or school. For this to happen, we must find time to talk and share. Principals may have limited resources, but they are often very resourceful. If included in the conversation loop, they may be able to carve out niches of time for teachers to work together on important projects, like improving student knowledge of spelling.

The number of articles on spelling being published for school principals attests to their interest. Include principals when student papers are being analyzed for types of spelling problems. Converse with them when possible strategies are being investigated for use in minilessons. Work with them as you and other faculty members establish realistic goals for spelling improvement, and plan with them ways to take your achievements public.

Consider inviting to the school a local education reporter who may be able to help share the results of your work with the wider public. Get on the agenda of a school board meeting and include both parent and student voices in your report of your successes. Be sure to focus on instructional improvement results at open houses and parent meetings. Teachers are often reluctant to toot their own horns, but they need to work at informative self-promotion when their work warrants it. Even moderate successes should be shared beyond the classroom—with parents, superintendents, and school boards.

Commitment, Time, and Support

Many schools and districts have a short attention span, and as the Ann Arbor teacher reminded us at the beginning of this chapter, lasting change takes time. One year's new initiatives often seem to be followed by a dozen more the very next year. We advocate a kinder, gentler approach: limiting goals for spelling, particularly as changes are begun.

Remember, research on change suggests it will take at least three years to feel totally comfortable with a schoolwide change and to see sustainable results. If teachers decide to begin with a focus on high-frequency words, help students identify the words they use most often in their writing. Because the high-frequency words students use in science and social studies may vary from those they use frequently in English, specialty area vocabulary should become part of the list of words students are expected to write often. In any content area, many of the same strategies will be helpful.

As discussed earlier, you and other teachers may agree to have students maintain personal dictionaries, keep spelling logs, or create mnemonic devices to help them remember the spelling of particular words. Regardless of the focus selected, consistency of expectations and strategies will reinforce the importance of correct spelling and show students that spelling counts.

Because results of change may be difficult to detect, decide in advance how long you will continue with your new curriculum approach before you revisit your decision. We hope you'll feel comfortable promising yourself to stay with your new approach for at least a year. If yours is a departmental or schoolwide change, make formal agreements with others to continue the project for at least a full school year before reassessing its effectiveness. You'll also want to decide in advance what types of data you'll collect to measure effectiveness. Figure 12–3 offers a guide for setting up a system to assess student progress. Earlier chapters discussed using spelling histories from challenged spellers as artifacts that document changes in both the affective level as well as the cognitive level.

Throughout the first year, you may want to collect periodic samples of first draft and polished draft writings so that you can examine individual student progress in authentic situations. You may want to examine how the types of errors students make change during the year. It's likely that becoming aware of spelling

---

- Collect samples of students' first and final draft writing periodically throughout the first year.
- Interview challenged spellers from time to time to assess attitudinal changes.
- Review artifacts, looking for signs of growth in proficiency, use of more challenging words, and willingness to take ownership of spelling as a part of writing.
- Make new goals for the next year. Determine the types of minilessons that will be needed to promote additional growth.
- Think about new questions. What would you like to learn about supporting student growth in spelling next year?

Figure 12–3. Assessing Progress

and their own spelling processes will help students improve some of the types of errors first noticed. With a stronger sense of process, students may begin to take more risks with sophisticated vocabulary, which may lead initially to new types of errors on those new words. This cycle of risk taking–gradually gaining control–risk taking is a positive step for most students. Particularly if minilessons focus on roots, prefixes, and suffixes as described earlier, you may find students are more inclined to experiment. If words end up on word walls or in special personalized dictionaries, successful use of more sophisticated vocabulary in written work is likely.

Because of the enormous amount of baggage challenged spellers bring to writing, you may want to conduct a few interviews during that first year to gauge students' attitudes about spelling and to be able to sense changes in their attitudes as you move through the year. Helping students feel less fearful of spelling and more prepared with strategies to self-edit their work will build competence and confidence in writing, offering them a sense of power that many have not experienced before.

After the first year, try to arrange for time so you and your colleagues can examine artifacts collected with the eyes of teacher researchers. Ask yourself what you notice from the papers, interviews, portfolios, or other artifacts.

What do you note about student attitudes?
Do you sense an increase in student ownership of their language in final drafts?
Do they appear to have new strategies that they can bring to bear when editing for a final paper?

We believe you'll see positive changes.

During this process of revisiting your spelling innovations, you'll have a golden opportunity to analyze the new types of errors students are making and think about additional changes you may wish to add the next year. If you've focused on teaching rules that generalize and working to raise awareness of high-frequency words, you may add an emphasis on roots, suffixes, and prefixes. In doing so you will be able to help students learn to crack the code for some difficult words and simultaneously learn how to build interesting new vocabulary that will enrich their writing. We hope the ideas suggested in Parts 2 and 3 of this book will support your thinking.

13

Thinking About a Policy for Spelling

As students move across classrooms and disciplines, they are apt to experience widely varying expectations for spelling. One teacher might allow multiple drafts before final copies are collected, permitting students to draw upon available resources to correct spelling. Another may grade first draft writing completed in class and deduct points for every spelling error. Sometimes, teachers in disciplines other than English will even consider spelling an English skill and ignore it altogether or simply expect compliance.

Such a variety of expectations will likely confuse students about the significance of spelling in the world beyond school. Schoolwide conversations about spelling would establish common expectations and strategies for reinforcing spelling skills and, in effect, create a spelling policy. A thoughtful and supportive schoolwide policy provides a consistency of expectations, making it possible for teachers to work as a cohesive unit in supporting spelling growth.

However, before implementing such a schoolwide spelling policy, careful and thoughtful deliberation is required: What is to be gained? When and where is spelling important? Why are particular approaches better than others? How will challenged spellers be accommodated within the system of common expectations?

What's to Be Gained?

Perhaps the most important single gain realized from a spelling policy is an agreement to help spellers achieve, even if they have consistently struggled in the past. Too often, emphasis on spelling has translated to checking papers and deducting points when misspelled words are found. We advocate a very different approach, one that consistently emphasizes the importance of spelling in final draft writing, provides resources and strategies taught in English classes and reinforced in all other classes, and eliminates penalties for spelling errors in first draft writing, including writing done under test situations. This type of policy communicates clearly that spelling is important in writing that is public and that we need to develop an array of strategies and tools to address our students' spelling needs.

Though consistent, thoughtful instructional policies are difficult to achieve, they are extremely beneficial on a number of levels. Policies that work require faculty and administrators to engage in focused conversations that

- broaden their base of information about a particular issue,
- examine the actual problems in evidence among their students,
- consider the impact of possible policy guidelines for *all* students,
- plan for strategies to support all students in being successful with the new expectations, and
- communicate the new policy, its rationale, and its implementation strategies to various constituencies.

It's imperative that any policy support all students in meeting higher standards without placing unfair obstacles in the paths of some.

Perhaps the greatest benefit of a schoolwide policy is the emphasis it places on really understanding the problems students experience. To support conversations leading to spelling policy development and implementation, teachers will engage in fact finding about the extent of the problem, information gathering to understand how to solve the problem, and consideration of practices to support implementation. As noted earlier, starting with achievable goals—such as concentrating on specific high-frequency words and rules—makes it possible for students to experience, possibly for the first time, common expectations across all their classes. Think of the difference that might be evidenced in student writing if the most troublesome of the fifty words frequently misspelled by students were emphasized in all classes for a year. Just those fifty words could make a world of difference in student writing!

What if the policy also addressed issues of first and final draft writing? In some classes students already have opportunities to revise and edit work that will be graded for spelling and mechanics as well as content, organization, and other features. If we include clear language in our spelling policy about when spelling counts and the types of strategies and resources that students can count on for specific types of writing tasks, we again help to clarify issues of spelling while also emphasizing important features of writing instruction.

When Spelling Counts

As you begin to think about spelling expectations across the school, you must think carefully about when—and under what conditions—spelling will count. Regardless of whether a piece of writing is completed for an English class or a biology class, first draft writing seems to be an inappropriate time to be concerned about spelling. In first drafts, writers are trying, first and foremost, to get their ideas on paper. In content-rich classes, those ideas may include important information that requires use of words that are new to students (e.g., *longitude, latitude, democracy, anarchy, oligarchy, literary criticism, reciprocity*). Vocabulary words like these require students to concentrate on definitions, making meaningful connections as they attempt to integrate new concepts into the broader fabric of their knowledge. When grappling with new concepts, students may even be more prone to making errors with words they typically spell correctly. Particularly for students who already struggle with spelling, we must be careful not to allow the burden of correctly spelling words to negatively affect their success in demonstrating conceptual and informational knowledge.

For writing that is intended to be graded—final draft writing—opportunities for revision and editing are important. Obviously, writing completed in test situations will not have the benefit of revision and editing. While it is entirely realistic to require students to turn in written work that is spelled correctly in final draft writing, holding students accountable for spelling in test writing circumstances creates substantial obstacles for challenged spellers. Most of us have heard the litany "But in the real world . . ." followed by an emphasis on how correct spelling is a must and how dictionaries and other tools aren't always available. However, we might ask those individuals to think back—and think hard—about their own workplace writing. Writing that is ready for a public audience is usually completed after opportunities for revision and editing. Seldom are we required to produce *public writing* under pressure, without time or opportunity to look up a word, substitute another word, or ask a colleague about spelling.

Not only do we want students to understand that spelling is important, but we also want them to understand when and where it is important. As essential as spelling is in writing that is to be shared with a public audience, it is virtually unimportant in personal writing and minimally important in writing that is intended for an audience of friends. If spelling interferes with meaning, then it is a matter for concern; otherwise, for genres written for a personal audience, spelling is a minimally important skill. This is a critical distinction for students to make.

Approaches to Spelling

How can teachers in content areas support student revision and editing processes, addressing concerns like spelling, when they aren't trained as writing teachers? Content area teachers draw upon particular strategies and approaches in their content areas that help them write successfully in the genres characteristic of their fields of study. Helping teachers think about the processes they use and the types of writing that are important in their areas will support them in thinking about when and how mechanics (such as capitalization and punctuation) and spelling take on significance in their fields (see suggestions in Figure 13–1).

Many students are already allowed a process approach to writing in their English classes. That knowledge will be easily transferred into other content areas. Inservice and professional conversations that illustrate writing as a process will support these efforts. Conversations about process lead naturally to thinking about writing and learning across the curriculum. Because types of writing are specific to a discipline, sometimes varying by genre and purpose, supporting students in acquiring the appropriate strategies for writing like a scientist, a geographer, or a historian will help them gain success in that discipline. In formal writing within a discipline, nonwriting teachers should help students gain a mental model of the writing required.

Mental models are acquired best through experience with the genre. Giving students a sample of well-written student work and going through the sample with them to identify strong characteristics of the writing promotes understanding of structure, organization, voice, use of vocabulary, and appropriateness of conventions for final draft work. Creating opportunities for response—either by having

---

- Post high-frequency words that are emphasized by the entire school.
- Post high-use vocabulary for individual content areas.
- Grade for spelling only in final draft work after opportunities for revision and editing are provided.
- Refrain from grading for spelling when students are writing under test conditions.
- Highlight two to four words that students tend to misspell frequently in a particular paper.
- Require students to complete personal spelling logs and to register the words in their personal dictionaries.

Figure 13–1. Strategies to Support Spelling in All Classrooms

students read and ask questions about each other's work, having a student read her own paper aloud to herself and write about it reflectively, or having students meet briefly with the teacher—tends to improve the overall quality of the papers students write.

All of the writing strategies mentioned here help focus attention on correctness. Emphasizing for students what types of work will be graded for correctness helps them understand that in final draft writing, spelling counts. However, we must still be realistic about how much it counts. Is spelling valued more than content? More than organization? We hope not. Spelling is a small part of the overall mechanics of writing, as are capitalization and punctuation. As discussed in Chapter 11, rubrics provide excellent tools for helping students and teachers keep spelling in perspective (see Appendix G for a reproducible rubric).

Accommodating Challenged Spellers

In our efforts to support all students as they grow in spelling confidence and competence, it is especially important to remember how difficult spelling has been for some students. Practices that further frustrate and penalize these students for an area of weakness are the last thing we would suggest. We know that harsh penalties for spelling neither promote growth nor build confidence, so it is especially important to think about spelling policies with an eye toward supporting challenged spellers through positive instructional practices, holding them to realistic expectations, and avoiding undue penalties.

For formal pieces of writing—reports, essays, and narratives, among a host of genres—young writers should be held accountable for spelling and allowed to draw on a full array of strategies and resources. For other types of writing—writing intended to help students think about and through content matter—mechanics tend to be far less important. Learning logs, journals, and quick writes, such as entrance and exit slips, promote thinking and connections to previous knowledge. Most of the time the audience for such writing is one's self, and the writing is only graded for completion.

But what about those circumstances when students are required to complete first draft papers that are then evaluated? On many state writing assessments, provisions are in place for at least limited revision and editing. In other cases, we probably need to be honest with our students, talking with them frankly about what we do when confronted with a public writing performance with no opportunity to edit or no resources to support editing efforts. In interviews with good spellers, we repeatedly hear of have-a-go strategies, substituting a familiar word to replace an unknown one, and blurring handwriting to disguise misspellings. Of course we don't advocate poor handwriting, but being honest with our students about the fact that many writers find themselves in the same dilemma with spelling under test circumstances may help challenged spellers feel less self-critical and relax a little. Moreover, just knowing that many writers do substitute words or try several spellings before going with the one that looks best may help challenged spellers feel more capable and empowered as writers in stressful circumstances.

Creating Your Spelling Policy

Now that you have done your homework and understand as much as you can about the extent of your students' spelling proficiencies and difficulties, you are ready to craft a policy for your students, your department, or your school. Here is a sample policy statement that may serve as a starting point as you begin crafting your own.

Spelling Policy

Spelling is a skill that is important in the world beyond school. Correct spelling is considered a matter of courtesy in written expression. In writing intended for public audiences, we may be judged by others if our spelling is careless or inaccurate. Spelling matters in writing that is intended for public audiences. Correct spelling helps our readers focus on our message—not our spelling.

Because we feel that spelling is an important skill, we agree to support this policy in our school. Spelling will be addressed uniformly in all of our classrooms. We intend to provide a supportive, nurturing environment for all students to grow as speller and writers. Therefore we will work to implement the following practices in all classrooms:

- High-frequency words are essential to everyday writing. Lists of high-frequency words will be posted in every classroom. Students are to review these lists and refer to them while writing. High-frequency words from these lists should be spelled correctly all the time.
- In writing that is considered *first draft* or *writing to learn*—like journals, logs, and notes—spelling will not be graded.
- In writing that is considered *final draft*, students will be given opportunities to write more than one draft and receive feedback from peers and/or the teacher. In final draft papers, spelling will be considered in accordance with the rubric established in the particular class.
- Students will be expected to maintain and use personal dictionaries and spelling logs for words that are troublesome in each discipline.
- Students will be encouraged to use a variety of tools to think about the words they misspell, to reflect upon why they misspell them, and to decide upon strategies or cues to help spell them correctly in the future.

A policy must reflect the individuals who will be affected by it. Voices of teachers, parents, and students should be considered as a policy is crafted and adopted. Effective policies support student growth, remove barriers, and invite continuous examination of practice.

A Speller's Bill of Rights

Challenged spellers in middle school and high school classes have often been victimized by their spelling difficulties. By building their awareness of strategies and tools, embedding spelling practice in real writing, and providing solid instruction in the writing process, teachers can help all students grow in their competence as spellers and writers. At the Spring Conference of the National Council of Teachers of English in 1996, Sandra Wilde presented A Speller's Bill of Rights. Wilde's work has focused largely on elementary-aged children. Nonetheless, many of her findings apply equally well to older learners. Here's her bill of rights:

As a speller, you have . . .

1. the right to express yourself in first-draft writing regardless of what words you do and don't know how to spell.
2. the right to do a lot of reading, which is probably the greatest single factor in spelling acquisition.
3. the right to actively construct knowledge about the spelling system.
4. the right to learn that spelling does matter.
5. the right to developmentally appropriate education in spelling.
6. the right to know about and have available a lot of ways to come up with spellings.
7. the right to learn how to proofread.
8. the right to have spelling placed in its proper context as a small piece of the writing and language-learning process.
9. the right to be valued as a human being regardless of your spelling.

Through our instructional practice, we strive to extend these rights to all of our students.

You Know It Works When . . .

It's more than just test scores. It's the way my students talk about spelling. It's the way their confidence has increased. It's all about their new sense of power over their written language.

KAREN

14

Evidence of Success

"We should do this every day," Mike remarked as he picked up his books and walked off to fourth hour. I was stunned. Did he really just say that? I was used to those comments on movie day or even silent reading day, but not on days when we concentrated on spelling!

We spent the period brainstorming and listing spelling strategies we knew. Students who were good spellers had the opportunity to share the wealth represented by their large bank of strategies with others who had few to support them. Challenged spellers, who seemed only able to recite *i* before *e* except after *c*, shared their knowledge as well while benefiting from the group experience. Our sharing moved seamlessly into a discussion of what to do when you can't remember how to spell a certain word.

"I can never remember how to spell *tomorrow*. I always get it wrong. Is it one *m* or two?" Sarah directed her question to the whole class.

"It's one *m*," Adam told her.

I could see the rest of the students either thinking about it in their heads or writing the word on their desks with their fingers.

"I always think of *tomorrow* as like *sorrow*. There's only one *s* where the *m* would be and two *r*s just like *tomorrow*. I don't know if it will work for you, but that's how I always remember it."

As the conversation continued, hands raised from all over as they tried to think of tricks to remember trouble words. This spelling lesson had all the things kids love: they were able to talk to each other; they were challenged because there was no single right way; and they got to be teachers and help each other out. It had all the makings for a great lesson, and it was on spelling!

This was one of the challenges our research group faced: How could we teach spelling in interesting and meaningful ways so that kids could actually use and remember the information later in their writing? As a group, we brainstormed possible strategies and lessons for our students' spelling problems and word demons. Armed with these tools, we headed back into our classrooms to see if they would help our students' writing.

Our minilessons focused on the core understanding we discussed in Part 2. These strategies and activities were structured to support whole-class, small-group, and individual spelling learning that could be immediately applied to writing. What we found from our project is simply this: focused, supportive work with spelling produces results. We have witnessed improvements in our students' spelling in actual writing. Moreover, we have observed radical changes in student attitudes about spelling, in terms of both their interest and enthusiasm as well as their willingness to take ownership and risks. We've documented these findings in a number of formal and informal ways, including observations and teacher participant-observer journals, student self-reports, and products students have provided.

Observed Changes

Throughout the year, we document changes we observe in our students' spelling and spelling habits. These observations help us become aware of changes in students' attitudes about spelling and writing. Once students become aware of their own spelling processes and learn to depend on strategies that they can control, a noticeable shift in attitude follows. No one likes to be a victim. Knowing how to consciously approach spelling, leading to correctly spelled papers, is empowering. Where before, many of our most challenged spellers would hesitate to engage in writing, now they are more willing to take risks with their pieces, no longer allowing spelling to overshadow the messages they wish to present. As students have taken more responsibility for their own spelling, they have exhibited a stronger investment in their own written voices.

Tracy observes that she is "no longer a personal dictionary" who responds constantly to her students' shared question: "How do you spell this?" Instead, by using student questions about words as a platform for teaching or rehearsing a strategy, she has noted a steady increase in their abilities to answer their own questions, drawing from the wealth of strategies she has provided. Instead of feeling lost in the clutter of spelling errors, students are now able to circle words that look funny. And, they are able to do this regardless of their original spelling level.

Recognizing that a word is incorrectly spelled is a major step for most challenged spellers. Once that has been accomplished, it becomes a straightforward process to work through strategies that the student has already learned. If that fails, other strategies are available to provide external assistance, such as the use of peer editors. Rather than relying on the teacher as an editor or fearing citation by the word police, students own their processes and their strategies.

For spelling, the success of any program rests in the success of final draft writing. In all of our classrooms, we have witnessed an increase in student competency in spelling on final draft papers. Clearly, this relates to both a raised student awareness of the importance of the writing process and an expanded repertoire of strategies. For writing that counts, our students know we expect them to revise and edit. They also know that we are minimally concerned with spelling in early drafts. In early drafts we are reading for ideas, development, and flow. When drafts are shaped into products that are intended for a public audience, then students draw upon strategies for addressing troublesome words. Now, because of the minilessons and practice they have experienced, they know these strategies.

In follow-up placement testing, most of the students we tested scored higher than they had in original testing. Two things are important to note here, however. First, we continue to be far less concerned about test scores than spelling in final draft writing. Tests require that students produce correctly spelled words out of context and without use of the strategies we have worked so hard to teach. In our opinion, that sends a contradictory message to the students: *Use these strategies because they are important; however, when it really counts, you won't have them available*. For the Category Three and Four students, that message may be all it takes to discourage them from taking minilessons seriously. Second, as we have found repeatedly, low scores on tests do not necessarily mean that our students have failed to internalize spelling strategies. Only when we correlate findings from test scores with findings from final draft writing are we able to make accurate judgments about what our students have learned. For our purposes, looking at final drafts collected early, midway, and later in the term and completing a quick error analysis for each provides the most useful information about student spelling growth. From this data, we have observed improvement in student spelling competency and confidence. What's more important, however, is that our students have observed this as well.

Student Self-Reports

Students began to self-report improvements in spelling as early as their first quarterly portfolios. In Jennifer's class, for example, students set goals for each quarter and reflect on their learning at the end. She noticed that quarter reflections began to indicate a desire to make spelling improvements. Students were also required to tell her how they planned to achieve those established spelling goals. By the second quarter, students were already noting that they were using spelling rules and homonym cards to assist them in checking for correct spelling. Frequently misspelled word lists were also mentioned as a helpful tool for students to learn and use conventional spelling.

Challenged spellers in our classes report that they feel more comfortable with spelling, because they now know everyone has some areas of weakness or words they stumble on. They love the way they can now help each other. Students know they won't be subjected to weekly quizzes on words or be made to memorize an obscure list each week. Spelling is no longer a separate subject divorced from writing. Our students know that spelling matters: It matters because they have significant things to say, and when they write those things down, spelling helps readers understand the messages they want to communicate. For public writing, spelling takes on real significance.

Students demonstrate a heightened awareness of words. We post words in alphabetical order all over the walls, and students end up using the walls both for spelling assistance and to incorporate some new words into their language. Karen has overheard students tossing around new words while walking around the halls, saying things like, "You are such an *anomaly*." Because students have seen words for months, played with them formally and informally, and incorporated them into their writing, they report a heightened sense of excitement and investment with words.

Jennifer and others structure student-led conferences as a platform for parent-teacher conferences. During these sessions, students take the lead in discussing their work and progress with their parents and teacher(s). As students describe their portfolios and the types of writing with which they have worked over the course of the quarter or semester, they often talk about their own awareness of their improved spelling. Where spelling was previously an area that elicited apologies and denials, it now has become an area in which students express pride—about both their new knowledge of spelling and their sense of power to create correctly spelled texts.

Student-Generated Products

Jennifer's students end each year by inviting their parents, guardians, grandparents, or other family members to a Portfolio Night, a student-led conference that focuses on their learning, reading, and writing over the course of the entire year. The portfolio is full of a student's best pieces of writing, in final draft form: best journal entries and literary logs; a comprehensive yearlong list of reading and writing; and a lengthy self-reflection in the areas of reading and writing. At the end of the conference, parents fill out a comment sheet for Jennifer to read. This is usually the last piece of writing she gets from parents about their observations of their children's learning and the improvements they have seen. This year, the mother of a struggling speller noted that she had seen his spelling improve during eighth grade and credited Jennifer's consistent emphasis on spelling through minilessons, coaching of writing, and high expectations as the reasons for the change. Such observations are common now as parental awareness of spelling strategies is raised. Generally, parents are thrilled to observe increased investment in writing—and spelling—in their children.

A Note About Standardized Tests

Many schools are asked to prove the spelling abilities of students through the use of standardized achievement tests. Most of us who teach recognize the problematic nature of making educational decisions based on these tests, particularly if standardized test scores are the only data being examined. Obviously, standardized tests represent the worst practice for challenged spellers. They test students on words outside of the context of writing. They judge spelling based on tests taken under pressure and without resources. They may not even focus on words that students have studied or used at all.

Many standardized achievement tests are multiple choice. Students are generally given a word spelled four different ways and must select the correct spelling. For students with strong visual memory, this is typically a straightforward task. For others, however, we must remember that the cueing system they are most apt to use is sound. These students tend to look at the four words, sound them out, and make a selection. If you have the opportunity to examine multiple-choice spelling tests, you'll probably find that some of the choices for each item are phonetical possibilities. In its simplest form, this could mean that the choices for *variable* are presented as follows:

veriable   varible
vareible   variable

In theory, if students have mastered the types of rules appropriate for various levels—in this case the *-able/-ible* rule—they should be able to apply the rules and determine the correct spelling. However, this test item has more going on than one rule will address. Regardless of the score students make on this item, we still have little idea whether they can actually spell the word in their writing, whether their difficulty is based on pronunciation difficulties instead of a lack of meaning-based knowledge, or whether they were confused by the close proximity of the words spelled with slight differences.

Strategies like have-a-go, where students practice writing words multiple times to determine the correct spelling, will help prepare students for these tests. Further, careful analysis of the types of skills and rules being tested on grade-level tests will allow us to be more strategic in the types of information we include in minilessons for students. And, even though it is risky business to offer practice in methods we feel are faulty, we may need to allow some time for students to practice taking tests of this kind, particularly if judgments about the student, the program, or the school will be made as a result of a single measure.

Without student writing samples, we know little more about the students' spelling than we did before the test. It is an unfortunate reality for schools today that instructional policy decisions are often made on the basis of data like that gleaned from standardized achievement tests taken in isolation. There's no easy solution to this dilemma. It is imperative that we increase conversation on as many levels as possible to help parents, legislators, and the general public understand why assessments of spelling within the context of student writing are a better and more informative way of gathering information upon which to make decisions.

Forward Glances

When we teach with a reflective, critical eye, we always examine current practices to raise questions for further exploration. In our case, spelling will probably always be a ministudy as we look back at the lessons we've offered across the previous year, the atmosphere for writing that we've orchestrated, and the expectations for spelling and language ownership that we've worked hard to build. As secondary teachers, we have limited time with our students, sometimes as little as one period a day for one semester. Obviously, we hold no claim to reorienting all of our challenged spellers and certainly we would never suggest that we could make the challenge faced by some students go away.

Nonetheless, we have witnessed real changes in student attitude and competence engendered by a soft, consistent emphasis on word awareness. Emphasizing spelling instruction and strategies in minilessons, weaving it into the fabric of the writing process, and providing consistent support and coaching have paid off in our classes. Now, our questions are different.

Our minilessons cover many of the concerns raised by our students' writing and early placement tests. These lessons cover both broad areas of concern and very specific strategies. Some, like root word study, encompass numerous subparts that potentially lead to dozens of new lessons across a year. Others, like proofreading, may lead to introductory strategies that are later emphasized in conferences and subsequent whole-group discussions.

As we look back across a year's or a semester's instruction, we revisit our students writing, identify areas where growth has not been achieved, and ask: *What next? What new minilessons do I need to create for next year to address this concern or need?* Spelling instruction, like teaching itself, is an evolving art. As lifelong teacher researchers, we learn from what we've done so that we can do it better. Our students are our teachers; they help us see what they need to continue their growth.

VI

Tools, Resources, and Information

Exploring Your Spelling History

Spelling has been a part of your school experience for a long time. Every time you sit down to write, you draw upon your knowledge of spelling. As we get started this term, I would like for us to explore together your spelling background. What do you remember about learning to spell? How did you learn to spell words at school? At home? What kinds of things did your teachers, parents, and other important people do to help teach you spelling? What do you think are your strengths in spelling? What do you think are your weaknesses? How do you feel about your spelling now?

Use any tools you are accustomed to using. Please write a rough draft (no polishing allowed on this one). It will be helpful if this paper is handwritten. I'll be looking at these papers to see the types of errors you tend to make, the types of instruction that seem to work best for you, and the types of minilessons I may want to teach.

In addition to the questions above, you may want to think about these aspects of your spelling history:

- your early memories of spelling
- spelling in school
- other people's attitudes about spelling (teachers, parents, peers)
- your attitudes about spelling

Error Analysis Chart

Student name:

Writing sample:

Total words:

Total incorrect: Total duplicates:

Homophones/wrong words   Faulty grammatical knowledge

Structural and pronunciation concerns   Prefix/suffix errors

Incorrect splitting or joining of words

Spelling Conference Log

Student:

Date:

Writing sample:

Notes for study:

1

2

3

4

5

6

7

For extra help, add any of the words above to your personal spelling log.

Spelling Log A

Correct spelling of the word:

Why do you think you misspelled the word?

What kind of word is it?

Correct spelling of the word:

Why do you think you misspelled the word?

What kind of word is it?

Correct spelling of the word:

Why do you think you misspelled the word?

What kind of word is it?

Spelling Log B

Student name:

Misspelled Word   Correct Spelling   Error Analysis

_____   _____   _____

Strategy to try:

_____

Misspelled Word   Correct Spelling   Error Analysis

_____   _____   _____

Strategy to try:

_____

Misspelled Word   Correct Spelling   Error Analysis

_____   _____   _____

Strategy to try:

_____

Misspelled Word   Correct Spelling   Error Analysis

_____   _____   _____

Strategy to try:

_____

Prefixes, Suffixes, and Roots

Building Knowledge with Prefixes

a, an	not or without	atypical
		apathy
		atom
		atrophy
		_____
		_____

ab, abs, a	from or away	absent
		avoid
		abnormal
		_____
		_____

ambi, amb	both or around	ambidextrous
		ambiguous
		amphibious
		_____
		_____

bi, bis, bin	both, double, twice	bicycle
		binoculars
		biannual
		_____
		_____

extra, extro	beyond, outside	extraterrestrial
		extrovert
		extinguish
		_____
		_____

intro	into, inward	introvert
		introduce
		insight
		_____
		_____

mis	incorrect, bad	misprint
		misinterpret
		misrepresent
		_____
		_____

pre	before	preview
		pretext
		prevent
		_____
		_____

Other Interesting Prefixes to Explore

amphi	on both sides	amphibious, amphibians, amphitheater
ante	before, in front of	antebellum, antecedent, antechamber
anti	against, opposing	antidote, anti-aircraft, anticlimax
be	near, more	before, beneath, belittle
by	side, close, near	bypass, bylaw, byline
co, con	together, with	cooperate, confidence, co-pilot
deca	ten	decade, decagon, decaliter
di	two, twice	divide, dilute, dichromatic
dis, dif	apart, away	disappear, diffuse, disclaim
ex	out of, from	expel, exceed, ex-president
hemi, semi	half	semicircle, hemisphere, semiconscious
infra	below, within	infrastructure, infrahuman, infrasonic
mal	badly, poorly	maladjusted, malnourished, malformed
meta, met	among, after, with	metabolic, metaphor, metaphysical
mono	one	monochrome, monopoly, monotone
non	not	nontoxic, nontaxable, nonexistent
oct, octa	eight	October, octagonal, octave

para	beside	paralegal, paraprofessional, parasite
poly	many	polygon, polyester, polychrome
post	after	postdepression, posterior, postoperative
re	back, again	return, renew, review
self	by oneself	self-sufficient, selfish, self-assured
trans, tra	across, beyond	transcontinental, transfer, transcend
un	not, release	unpleasant, unkind, unhappy
under	beneath, below	undervalue, underway, underwater

Note: when a prefix ends with a vowel and the base word begins with a vowel, a hyphen is often used.

Suffixes to Explore

able, ible	able, can do	capable, manageable, visible
al	relating to	gradual, manual, natural
ance, ancy	action, process, state	assistance, allowance, reliance
ary, ery, ory	quality of, place where	crematory, sanctuary, scenery
ate	make or cause	create, mandate, segregate
cian	having a certain skill	magician, musician, clinician
crat	to rule	bureaucrat, aristocrat, democrat
cy	action or function	normalcy, hesitancy, reluctancy
ee	receives the action	attendee, nominee, retiree
er, or	one who	teacher, doctor, caregiver
er	more	greater, sadder, happier
hood	condition	sisterhood, manhood, statehood
ish	resembling	childish, squeamish, puckish
ism	system, condition	feudalism, communism, sexism
ize	make	publicize, democratize, idolize
less	without	sleepless, aimless, pointless
ly	like	happily, sadly, jovially
ment	state of	statement, amendment, judgment
ness	state of	sleeplessness, kindness, happiness
ology	study of	biology, geology, sociology
ship	quality, state	ownership, leadership, dictatorship
some	tending to	frolicsome, lonesome. troublesome
tude	state of	attitude, altitude, latitude
tude	state of, condition of	servitude, aptitude, gratitude
ward	in the direction of	northward, inward, forward

Roots to Explore

acri, acer	bitter	acid, acrid, acrimony
am, amor	love, liking	amiable, amorous, paramour
anni, annu	year	annual, anniversary, per annum
aud, aus	hear, listen	audible, auditorium, audacious
bibl	book	bibliography, bibliophile, biblical
bio	life	biology, biography, biosphere
carn	flesh	carnivore, incarnation, carnivorous
chrom	color	monochrome, polychrome, chrome
chron	time	chronology, synchronicity, chronicle
corp	body	corporation, corpulent, corpus
cycl, cyclo	wheel	bicycle, unicycle, cyclone
dic	say, speak	dictate, edict, diction
dox, doc	teach	orthodox, indoctrinate, document
graph, gram	write	telegram, autograph, monograph
man	hand	manual, manipulate, maneuver
medi	half way	medicate, mediate, median
mor, mort	death	immortal, mortality, mortuary
nov	new	nova, novella, novice
omni	all, every	omnipresent, omnivorous, omnipotent
path, pathy	feeling	empathy, antipathy, apathy
ped, pod	foot	pedestrian, pedestal, podiatrist
photo	light	photograph, photon, photoelectric
phobia	fear	claustrophobia, agoraphobia, acrophobia
simil, simul	like, resembling	similar, assimilate, simultaneous
tend	tendency	extend, pretend, tender

Excellent sources for information on prefixes, suffixes, and roots:

Allen, Janet. 1999. *Words, Words, Words*. York, ME: Stenhouse.
Snowball, Diane, and Faye Bolton. 1999. *Spelling K–8 Planning and Teaching*. York, ME: Stenhouse.

Writing Rubric

Ideas and Content	Organization	Conventions
5 This paper is clear, focused, and interesting. It holds the reader's attention. Relevant details enrich the central theme or story line.	5 The organization enhances and showcases the central idea or theme. The order, structure, or presentation is compelling and moves the reader through the text.	5 The writer shows a good grasp of standard writing conventions (e.g., grammar, capitalization, punctuation, usage, spelling, paragraphing) and uses them effectively.
3 This paper is clear and focused, even though the overall result may not be captivating. Support is attempted, but it may be limited.	3 The reader can readily follow what's being said, but the overall organization may sometimes be ineffective or too obvious.	3 Errors, while not overwhelming, begin to impair readability. While errors do not block meaning, they tend to be distracting.
1 This paper lacks a central idea or purpose or forces the reader to make inferences based on very sketchy details.	1 Organization is haphazard and disjointed. The writing lacks direction. Ideas, details, or events are loosely strung together.	1 Many errors in conventions distract the reader and make the text difficult to read.
Word Choice	**Sentence Fluency**	**Voice**
5 Words convey the intended message in an interesting, precise, and natural way. The writing is full and rich yet concise.	5 The writing has an easy flow and rhythm when read aloud. Sentences are well built with consistently strong and varied structures.	5 The writer speaks directly to the reader in a way that is individualistic, expressive, and engaging. Clearly, the writer is involved in the text and intends the writing to be read.
3 The language, though ordinary, conveys the message; though functional, it may lack excitement or "punch," resulting in a paper without flair.	3 Sentences tend to be mechanical rather than fluid. The text hums along efficiently for the most part.	3 The writer seems sincere but not fully involved in the topic. The result is pleasant, acceptable, sometimes even personal, but not compelling.
1 The writer struggles with a limited vocabulary, groping for words to convey meaning. Often the language is vague and abstract or redundant and devoid of details.	1 The paper is difficult to follow or to read aloud. Sentences tend to be choppy, incomplete, rambling, irregular, or just very awkward.	1 The writer seems wholly indifferent, uninvolved, or dispassionate. The writing is flat, lifeless, stiff, or mechanical.

Rubric modeled after the Northwest Lab's Six-Trait Assessment of Writing

Root Word Web

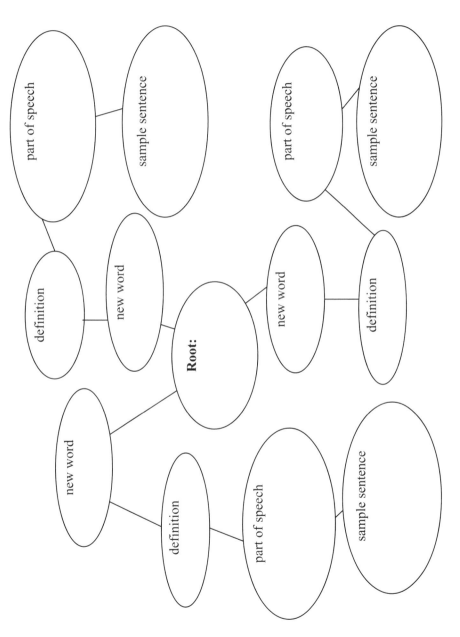

APPENDIX I

High-Frequency Words

High-frequency words for reading vary somewhat from those used for writing. We've included two different types of lists to support your planning.

Fry's 1,000 Instant Words

First Hundred

the	at	there	some	my
of	be	use	her	than
and	this	an	would	first
a	have	each	make	water
to	from	which	like	been
in	or	she	him	call
is	one	do	into	who
you	had	how	time	oil
that	by	their	has	its
it	word	if	look	now
he	but	will	two	find
was	not	up	more	long
for	what	other	write	down
on	all	about	go	day
are	were	out	see	did
as	we	many	number	get
with	when	then	no	come
his	your	them	way	made
they	can	these	could	may
I	said	so	people	part

Instant Two Hundred

over	name	boy	such	change
new	good	follow	because	off

146

sound	sentence	came	turn	play
take	man	want	here	spell
only	think	show	why	air
little	say	also	ask	away
work	great	around	went	animal
know	where	form	men	house
place	help	three	read	point
year	through	small	need	page
live	much	set	land	letter
me	before	put	different	mother
back	line	end	home	answer
give	right	does	us	found
most	too	another	move	study
very	mean	well	try	still
after	old	large	kind	learn
thing	any	must	hand	should
our	same	big	picture	America
just	tell	even	again	world

Instant Three Hundred

high	light	life	sea	watch
every	thought	always	began	far
near	head	those	grow	Indian
add	under	both	took	really
food	story	paper	river	almost
between	saw	together	four	let
own	left	got	carry	above
below	don't	group	state	girl
country	few	often	once	sometimes
plant	while	run	book	mountain
last	along	important	hear	cut
school	might	until	stop	young
father	close	children	without	talk
keep	something	side	second	soon
tree	seem	feet	later	list
never	next	car	miss	song
start	hard	mile	idea	being
city	open	night	enough	leave
earth	example	walk	eat	family
eye	begin	white	face	it's

Instant Four Hundred

body	usually	hours	five	cold
music	didn't	black	step	cried
color	friend	products	morning	plan
stand	easy	happened	passed	notice
sun	heard	whole	vowel	south
questions	order	measure	true	sing
fish	red	remember	hundred	war
area	door	early	against	ground
mark	sure	waves	pattern	fall
dog	become	reached	numeral	king
horse	top	listen	table	town
birds	ship	wind	north	I'll
problem	across	rock	slowly	unit
complete	today	space	money	figure
room	during	covered	map	certain
knew	short	fast	farm	field
since	better	several	pulled	travel
ever	best	hold	draw	wood
piece	however	himself	voice	fire
told	low	toward	seen	upon

Instant Five Hundred

done	front	stay	warm	object
English	feel	green	common	am
road	fact	known	bring	rule
halt	inches	island	explain	among
ten	street	week	dry	noun
fly	decided	less	though	power
gave	contain	machine	language	cannot
box	course	base	shape	able
finally	surface	ago	deep	six
wait	produce	stood	thousands	size
correct	building	plane	yes	dark
oh	ocean	system	clear	ball
quickly	class	behind	equation	material
person	note	ran	yet	special
became	nothing	round	government	heavy
shown	rest	boat	filled	fine

minutes	carefully	game	heat	pair
strong	scientists	force	full	circle
verb	inside	brought	hot	include
stars	wheels	understand	check	built

Instant Six Hundred

can't	region	window	arms	west
matter	return	difference	brother	lay
square	believe	distance	race	weather
syllables	dance	heart	present	root
perhaps	members	sit	beautiful	instruments
bill	picked	sum	store	meet
felt	simple	summer	job	third
suddenly	cells	wall	edge	months
test	paint	forest	past	paragraph
direction	mind	probably	sign	raised
center	love	legs	record	represent
farmers	cause	sat	finished	soft
ready	rain	main	discovered	whether
anything	exercise	winter	wild	clothes
divided	eggs	wide	happy	flowers
general	train	written	beside	shall
energy	blue	length	gone	teacher
subject	wish	reason	sky	held
Europe	drop	kept	glass	describe
moon	developed	interest	million	drive

Instant Seven Hundred

cross	buy	temperature	possible	fraction
speak	century	bright	gold	Africa
solve	outside	lead	milk	killed
appear	everything	everyone	quiet	melody
metal	tall	method	natural	bottom
son	already	section	lot	trip
either	instead	lake	stone	hole
ice	phrase	consonant	act	poor
sleep	soil	within	build	let's
village	bed	dictionary	middle	fight
factors	copy	hair	speed	surprise
result	free	age	count	French

jumped	hope	amount	cat	died
snow	spring	scale	someone	beat
ride	case	pounds	sail	exactly
care	laughed	although	rolled	remain
floor	nation	per	bear	dress
hill	quite	broken	wonder	iron
pushed	type	moment	smiled	couldn't
baby	themselves	tiny	angle	fingers

Instant Eight Hundred

row	grew	east	suppose	direct
least	skin	pay	woman	information
catch	valley	single	coast	serve
climbed	cents	touch	bank	child
wrote	key	period	desert	ring
shouted	president	express	wire	increase
continued	brown	mouth	choose	history
itself	trouble	yard	clean	cost
else	cool	equal	visit	maybe
plains	cloud	decimal	bit	business
gas	lost	yourself	whose	separate
England	sent	control	received	break
burning	symbols	practice	garden	uncle
design	wear	report	please	hunting
joined	bad	straight	strange	flow
foot	save	rise	caught	lady
law	experiment	statement	fell	students
ears	engine	stick	team	human
grass	alone	party	God	art
you're	drawing	seeds	captain	feeling

Instant Nine Hundred

supply	fit	sense	position	meat
corner	addition	string	entered	lifted
electric	belong	blow	fruit	process
insects	safe	famous	tied	army
crops	soldiers	value	rich	hat
tone	guess	wings	dollars	property
hit	silent	movement	send	particular
sand	trade	pole	sight	swim

doctor	rather	exciting	chief	terms
provide	compare	branches	Japanese	current
thus	crowd	thick	stream	park
won't	poem	blood	planets	sell
cook	enjoy	lie	rhythm	shoulder
bones	elements	spot	eight	industry
tail	indicate	bell	science	wash
board	except	fun	major	block
modern	expect	loud	observe	spread
compound	flat	consider	tube	cattle
mine	seven	suggested	necessary	wife
wasn't	interesting	thin	weight	sharp

Instant Words Ten Hundred

company	France	shoes	workers	rope
radio	repeated	actually	Washington	cotton
we'll	column	nose	Greek	apple
action	western	afraid	women	details
capital	church	dead	bought	entire
factories	sister	sugar	led	corn
settled	oxygen	adjective	march	substances
yellow	plural	fig	northern	smell
isn't	various	office	create	tools
southern	agreed	huge	British	conditions
truck	opposite	gun	difficult	cows
fair	wrong	similar	match	track
printed	chart	death	win	arrived
wouldn't	prepared	score	doesn't	located
ahead	pretty	forward	steel	sir
chance	solution	stretched	total	seat
born	fresh	experienced	deal	division
level	shop	rose	determine	effect
triangle	suffix	allow	evening	underline
molecules	especially	fear	nor	view

(Fry, Kress, and Fountoukidis 2000)

High-Frequency Writing Words

Rebecca Sitton identifies the following high-frequency words for writing.

1.	the	31.	but	61.	into
2.	of	32.	what	62.	has
3.	and	33.	all	63.	more
4.	a	34.	were	64.	her
5.	to	35.	when	65.	two
6.	in	36.	we	66.	like
7.	is	37.	there	67.	him
8.	you	38.	can	68.	see
9.	that	39.	an	69.	time
10.	it	40.	your	70.	could
11.	he	41.	which	71.	no
12.	for	42.	their	72.	make
13.	was	43.	said	73.	than
14.	on	44.	if	74.	first
15.	are	45.	do	75.	been
16.	as	46.	will	76.	its
17.	with	47.	each	77.	who
18.	his	48.	about	78.	now
19.	they	49.	how	79.	people
20.	at	50.	up	80.	my
21.	be	51.	out	81.	made
22.	this	52.	them	82.	over
23.	from	53.	then	83.	did
24.	I	54.	she	84.	down
25.	have	55.	many	85.	only
26.	or	56.	some	86.	way
27.	by	57.	so	87.	find
28.	one	58.	these	88.	use
29.	had	59.	would	89.	may
30.	not	60.	other	90.	water

91.	long	131.	place	171.	along
92.	little	132.	well	172.	while
93.	very	133.	such	173.	might
94.	after	134.	here	174.	next
95.	words	135.	take	175.	sound
96.	called	136.	why	176.	below
97.	just	137.	help	177.	saw
98.	where	138.	put	178.	something
99.	most	139.	different	179.	thought
100.	know	140.	away	180.	both
101.	get	141.	again	181.	few
102.	through	142.	off	182.	those
103.	back	143.	went	183.	always
104.	much	144.	old	184.	show
105.	go	145.	number	185.	large
106.	good	146.	great	186.	often
107.	new	147.	tell	187.	together
108.	write	148.	men	188.	ask
109.	our	149.	say	189.	house
110.	me	150.	small	190.	don't
111.	man	151.	every	191.	world
112.	too	152.	found	192.	going
113.	any	153.	still	193.	want
114.	day	154.	between	194.	school
115.	same	155.	name	195.	important
116.	right	156.	should	196.	until
117.	look	157.	home	197.	form
118.	think	158.	big	198.	food
119.	also	159.	give	199.	keep
120.	around	160.	air	200.	children
121.	another	161.	line	201.	feet
122.	came	162.	set	202.	land
123.	come	163.	own	203.	side
124.	work	164.	under	204.	without
125.	three	165.	read	205.	boy
126.	must	166.	last	206.	once
127.	because	167.	never	207.	animal
128.	does	168.	us	208.	life
129.	part	169.	left	209.	enough
130.	even	170.	end	210.	took

211.	four	251.	sure	291.	face
212.	head	252.	knew	292.	door
213.	above	253.	it's	293.	cut
214.	kind	254.	try	294.	done
215.	began	255.	told	295.	group
216.	almost	256.	young	296.	true
217.	live	257.	sun	297.	half
218.	page	258.	thing	298.	red
219.	got	259.	whole	299.	fish
220.	earth	260.	hear	300.	plants
221.	need	261.	example	301.	living
222.	far	262.	heard	302.	black
223.	hand	263.	several	303.	eat
224.	high	264.	change	304.	short
225.	year	265.	answer	305.	United States
226.	mother	266.	room	306.	run
227.	light	267.	sea	307.	book
228.	country	268.	against	308.	gave
229.	father	269.	top	309.	order
230.	let	270.	turned	310.	open
231.	night	271.	learn	311.	ground
232.	picture	272.	point	312.	cold
233.	being	273.	city	313.	really
234.	study	274.	play	314.	table
235.	second	275.	toward	315.	remember
236.	soon	276.	five	316.	tree
237.	story	277.	himself	317.	course
238.	since	278.	usually	318.	front
239.	white	279.	money	319.	American
240.	ever	280.	seen	320.	space
241.	paper	281.	didn't	321.	inside
242.	hard	282.	car	322.	ago
243.	near	283.	morning	323.	sad
244.	sentence	284.	I'm	324.	early
245.	better	285.	body	325.	I'll
246.	best	286.	upon	326.	learned
247.	across	287.	family	327.	brought
248.	during	288.	later	328.	close
249.	today	289.	turn	329.	nothing
250.	however	290.	move	330.	though

331. idea	371. state	411. already
332. before	372. list	412. warm
333. lived	373. stood	413. gone
334. became	374. hundred	414. finally
335. add	375. ten	415. summer
336. become	376. fast	416. understand
337. grow	377. felt	417. moon
338. draw	378. kept	418. animals
339. yet	379. notice	419. mind
340. less	380. can't	420. outside
341. wind	381. strong	421. power
342. behind	382. voice	422. problem
343. cannot	383. probably	423. longer
344. letter	384. area	424. winter
345. among	385. horse	425. deep
346. able	386. matter	426. heavy
347. dog	387. stand	427. carefully
348. shown	388. box	428. follow
349. mean	389. start	429. beautiful
350. English	390. that's	430. everyone
351. rest	391. class	431. leave
352. perhaps	392. piece	432. everything
353. certain	393. surface	433. game
354. six	394. river	434. system
355. feel	395. common	435. bring
356. fire	396. stop	436. watch
357. ready	397. am	437. shell
358. green	398. talk	438. dry
359. yes	399. whether	439. within
360. built	400. fine	440. floor
361. special	401. round	441. ice
362. ran	402. dark	442. ship
363. full	403. past	443. themselves
364. town	404. ball	444. begin
365. complete	405. girl	445. fact
366. oh	406. road	446. third
367. person	407. blue	447. quite
368. hot	408. instead	448. carry
369. anything	409. either	449. distance
370. hold	410. held	450. although

451. sat	468. walked	485. else
452. possible	469. main	486. gold
453. heart	470. someone	487. build
454. real	471. center	488. glass
455. simple	472. field	489. rock
456. snow	473. stay	490. tall
457. rain	474. itself	491. alone
458. suddenly	475. boat	492. bottom
459. easy	476. question	493. check
460. leaves	477. wide	494. reading
461. lay	478. least	495. fall
462. size	479. tiny	496. poor
463. wild	480. hour	497. map
464. weather	481. happened	498. friend
465. miss	482. foot	499. language
466. pattern	483. care	500. job
467. sky	484. low	

Appendix J

Spelling Rules Worth Knowing

Here are the rules our students use most.

Rules for Prefixes

Generally when a prefix is added to a word, do not drop a letter from either the base word or the prefix (*dis* + *approve* = *disapprove*). Exceptions include *ad-*, *com-*, and *in-*, which can be absorbed by the base word so that the last letter in the prefix changes to match the beginning consonant of the base word (as in *illegal* instead of *inlegal*).

Rules for *i* Before *e*

Write *i* before *e* (*fiery*, *friend*) except after *c* or when sounded like *a* as in *neighbor* and *weigh*. When the *ie* or *ei* is not pronounced *ee*, it is usually spelled *ei* (*reign*).

Rules for Plurals

When forming the plural of most words, just add *s*.
When forming the plural of a word that ends with a *y* that is preceded by a vowel, add *s* (as in *monkeys*, *turkeys*).
When forming the plural of a word that ends in an *o* that is preceded by a vowel, add *s* (as in *patio/patios*).
When forming the plural of a word that ends in an *o* that is preceded by a consonant, add *es* (as in *tomato/tomatoes*).

Rules for Suffixes

When a one-syllable word ends in a consonant preceded by one vowel, double the final consonant before adding a suffix that begins with a vowel (as in *run/running*). In a word with two or more syllables that ends with a consonant-vowel-consonant (CVC), double the final letter before adding a suffix beginning with a vowel if the final syllable is stressed (as in *commit/committed*). If the final syllable is not stressed, do not double the final letter (as in *cancel/canceled, blanket/blanketed*).

If a word ends with a silent *e*, drop the *e* before adding a suffix that begins with a vowel (as in *give/giving, take/taking*).

When adding a suffix to a word where *y* is the last letter in a word and the *y* is preceded by a consonant, change the *y* to *i* before adding any suffix except those beginning with *i* (as in *happy/happiness, happily*).

When adding the suffix *-ly* or *-ness*, do not change the spelling of the base word unless it ends in *y* (*careful/carefully, fond/fondness, gay/gaily*).

-ible and *-able*

If a root is not a complete word, add *-ible* (as in *visible, edible, illegible*).

If a root is a complete word, add *-able* (as in *suitable, dependable, workable*).

If a root is a complete word that ends in a silent *e*, drop the *e* and add *-able* (as in *advisable, likable, valuable*).

Exceptions to the *-ible/-able* rule occur when the final sound is the hard *g* or *c*. Then the suffix used is *-able* (as in *apply/applicable*).

-ion

If the root ends in *ct*, add *-ion* (*select/selection*).

If the root ends in *ss*, add *-ion* (*discussion/discussion*).

If the root ends in *te*, drop the *e* and add *-ion* (*educate/education*).

If the root ends in *it*, change the *t* to *s* and add *-ion* (*permit/permission*).

If the root ends in *vowel-d-e*, drop the *e*, change the *d* to *s*, and add *-ion* (*explode/explosion*).

(Richards 2002)

Ideas for Teaching Spelling Rules

Teaching the *i* Before *e* Except After *c* Rule

Make a list of words that fit the rule and words that are exceptions.

Fits the pattern	Exceptions to the pattern
receive	reign
chief	weigh
piece	neighbor
receipt	weird
deceive	seize
_____	_____
_____	_____
_____	_____
_____	_____
_____	_____

In a piece of your own writing, circle each of the words you used that fit the pattern. In the same piece of writing, draw a box around each of the words that you used that are exceptions to the rule.

Select the three exceptions that you think you use the most. Write them here.

_____   _____   _____

Finally, make up a sentence with these words that will help you remember the words. For example, three frequently used words from the list above that cause many people trouble are *seize, weird,* and *neighbor*. A sample sentence to help remember that these are all exceptions might be *My neighbor will seize the weird package.*

Now you try:

_____

Working with Suffixes

When a one-syllable word (*run*) ends in a consonant preceded by one vowel, double the final consonant before adding a suffix that begins with a vowel.

Examples		Find other examples	
run	running	_____	_____
run	runner	_____	_____
shop	shopping	_____	_____
slap	slapping	_____	_____

In a word with two or more syllables that ends with a consonant-vowel-consonant, double the final letter before adding a suffix beginning with a vowel if the final syllable is stressed. If the final syllable is not stressed, do not double the final letter.

CVC with final syllable stressed		**CVC with final syllable not stressed**	
commit	committed	cancel	canceled
begin	beginning	_____	_____
refer	referring	_____	_____
_____	_____	_____	_____

If a word ends with a silent *e*, drop the *e* before adding a suffix that begins with a vowel.

state	stating	use	using
exercise	exercising	notice	noticing
_____	_____	_____	_____
_____	_____	_____	_____

Look at your own writing. Circle or highlight words ending in a silent *e*. Be sure to drop the *e* before adding a suffix that starts with a vowel. Record troublesome words in your spelling log and be sure to note a strategy to help you remember the words in the future.

When *y* is the last letter in a word and the *y* is preceded by a consonant, change the *y* to *i*.

try	tried	silly	silliness
breezy	breezier	happy	happiest
_____	_____	_____	_____
_____	_____	_____	_____

Look at your own writing. Record troublesome words in your spelling log and be sure to note a strategy to help you remember the words in the future.

In a piece of your own writing, circle the words with suffixes that you use and that give you difficulty. Select three words that you would like to focus attention on. List each of the three in your spelling log and describe a strategy or rule to help you remember these in the future.

Plurals

When forming the plural of most words, just add *s*.

book	books	day	_____
tool	tools	week	_____
service	services	_____	_____

When *y* is the last letter in a word and the *y* is preceded by a consonant, change the *y* to *i* and add *es*.

Examples		Your turn	
lady	ladies	_____	_____
sky	skies	_____	_____
fry	fries	_____	_____

When forming the plural of a word that ends in an o that is preceded by a vowel, add *s*.

Examples		Your turn	
patio	patios	_____	_____
rodeo	rodeos	_____	_____
zoo	zoos	_____	_____

When forming the plural of a word that ends in an *o* that is preceded by a consonant, add *es*, as in *tomato/tomatoes*.

Examples		Your turn	
potato	potatoes	_____	_____
hero	heroes	_____	_____

Frequently Confused Homophones

If we eliminate words with alternative spellings and proper nouns, we find more than 2,000 homophones in English. Here are some of those we encounter most often.

ad, add	all, awl	allowed, aloud
altar, alter	arc, ark	ascent, assent
auger, augur	away, aweigh	bad, bade
bail, bale	bait, bate	ball, bawl
bare, bear	baring, bearing	baron, barren
be, bee	beau, bow	berth, birth
blew, blue	boars, bores	bold, bowled
borders, boarders	brake, break	bread, bred
brewed, brood	bridal, bridle	but, butt
buy, by, bye	cash, cache	callous, callus
cannon, canon	carat, carrot, karat	cast, caste
cell, sell	censer, censor	cereal, serial
chews, choose	cite, sight, site	clause, claws
coax, cokes	core, corps	crewed, crude
damn, dam	days, daze	descent, dissent
desert, dessert	died, dyed	dies, dyes
draft, draught	earns, urns	ensure, insure
fair, fare	feat, feet	flair, flare
flea, flee	flour, flower	for, fore, four
fouls, fowls	gage, gauge	gait, gate
guilt, gilt	grate, great	groan, grown
hall, haul	hangar, hanger	hart, heart
hay, hey	heal, heel	higher, hire
him, hymn	hoards, hordes	horse, hoarse
hole, whole	hoop, whoop	idle, idol
in, inn	jam, jamb	knead, need
knew, new	knight, night	knot, not
laps, lapse	know, no	leak, leek

liar, lyre
lessen, lesson
meat, meet, mete
mind, mined
morn, mourn
none, nun
pail, pale
peak, peek
pleas, please
pray, prey
rain, reign, rein
read, reed
rigger, rigor
root, route
rough, ruff
scene, seen
shake, sheik
so, sew, sow
stake, steak
straight, strait
tail, tale
their, there
to, too, two
told, tolled
wail, wale, whale
waived, waved
weak, week
wet, whet
wood, would

loan, lone
mail, male
medal, mettle
missed, mist
muscles, mussels
paced, paste
pair, pare, pear
peer, pier
plum, plumb
profit, prophet
raise, rays, raze
rest, wrest
right, write, rite
role, roll
rye, wry
seam, seem
shoe, shoo
soar, sore
stalk, stork
suite, sweet
team, teem
throne, thrown
toe, tow
vale, veil
waist, waste
war, wore
were, whir, whirr
who's, whose
yoke, yolk

loot, lute
manner, manor
mews, muse
mode, mowed
mussed, must
packed, pact
passed, past
plain, plane
pore, pour
rack, wrack
rap, wrap
review, revue
roe, row
rote, wrote
sail, sale
seamed, seemed
slay, sleigh
stair, stare
stationary, stationery
tacks, tax
tear, tier
tide, tied
tracked, tract
wade, weighed
wait, weight
wares, wears, where's
which, witch
won't, wont
your, you're

Appendix L

Annotated Bibliography of Helpful Resources

Books

Allen, Janet. 1999. *Words, Words, Words: Teaching Vocabulary in Grades 4–12.* York, ME: Stenhouse.

This is a great resource for teachers who are frustrated with the vocabulary development of their students. From the hilarious contemporary Dolch list (3) to the integral tie between reading and vocabulary, this book offers good advice for enriching vocabulary growth.

Bear, Donald R., Marcia Invernizzi, Shane Templeton, and Francine Johnston. 2000. *Words Their Way: Word Study for Phonics, Vocabulary, and Spelling Instruction.* Upper Saddle River, NJ: Prentice Hall.

This text is rich in theory and resources. The authors establish a rationale for word study, trace the stages of orthographic knowledge development from emergent through intermediate stages, and offer many suggestions for helping students learn appropriate information about spelling at each stage. Heavy emphasis is placed on word sorts as tools for learning patterns.

Boulton, Faye, and Diane Snowball. 1993. *Teaching Spelling: A Practical Resource.* Portsmouth, NH: Heinemann.

Describing the authors' work in schools in Australia, this publication explores factors necessary to achieving spelling competency, discusses a variety of assessment issues, and details practical activities for supporting children's understanding of sound-letter relationships and word structures.

Fitzsimmons, Robert J., and Bradley M. Loomer. 1977. *Spelling Research and Practice.* Iowa City: University of Iowa.

This one is heavy but worth the read. It examines historical research about the teaching of spelling, making a very strong case for paying attention to high-use words.

Gentry, J. Richard. 1997. *My Kid Can't Spell! Understanding and Assisting Your Child's Literacy Development.* Portsmouth, NH: Heinemann.

Written for parents, this book contains accessible information about spelling development, helpful placement inventories, and suggestions for parents who wish to support their children's spelling growth. Useful for teachers, too.

———. 1987. *Spel . . . Is a Four-Letter Word.* Portsmouth, NH: Heinemann.

Starting with a letter to one of his former teachers who judged him as a result of his spelling, Richard Gentry helps us glimpse the myths about poor spelling and poor spellers. In a mere fifty-four pages, he helps us see how spelling knowledge develops for children and makes a strong connection between spelling and purposeful writing.

Gentry, J. Richard, and Jean Wallace Gillet. 1993. *Teaching Kids to Spell.* Portsmouth, NH: Heinemann.

This short book explores the stages of invented spelling, the qualities of the expert speller, and workshop methods for teaching spelling. The appendix contains useful charts focusing on the origins of English words; prefixes, suffixes, and stems; word lists organized by sound or letter; the five hundred words most commonly found in children's writing; and the words most commonly misspelled in children's writing.

Henderson, Edmund H., and James W. Beers, editors. 1980. *Developmental and Cognitive Aspects of Learning to Spell: A Reflection of Word Knowledge.* Newark, DE: International Reading Association.

Weighty but worth it, this collection explores theory related to spelling and reading acquisition among young learners ranging from issues of concepts of word, to the relationship between dialect and spelling, to the relationship between word knowledge and reading disabilities.

Hughes, Margaret, and Dennis Searle. 1997. *The Violent E and Other Tricky Sounds.* York, ME: Stenhouse.

Based on their study of one group of children over eight years of school, this book provides insights into levels of spelling development, why children spell as they do, and the types of approaches that support spelling development.

Laminack, Lester L., and Katie Wood. 1996. *Spelling in Use: Looking Closely at Spelling in Whole Language Classrooms*. Urbana, IL: NCTE.

This helpful, short book explores the development of spelling within the context of purposeful writing in the elementary grades. The research and teaching ideas presented are grounded in real classroom observations.

Scott, Ruth. 1993. *Spelling: Sharing the Secrets*. Toronto, Canada: Gage.

As the name implies, this book provides strategies to help students understand sound, visual, and meaning-based clues for spelling. The author works with elementary-aged children and demonstrates methods for integrating spelling instruction into various disciplines.

Snowball, Diane, and Faye Bolton. 1999. *Spelling K–8 Planning and Teaching*. York, ME: Stenhouse.

The authors describe a developmental approach to spelling within the context of constructivist learning and encourage teachers to study the needs of their children when planning for instruction. This book contains many helpful supports for understanding the needs of children.

Periodicals

Voices from the Middle, March 2002, 9 (3). Urbana, IL: The National Council of Teachers of English.

This entire edition of the Middle School Section journal is devoted to spelling. Multiple authors provide a variety of useful information about the teaching of spelling.

Amberg, Elizabeth. 2000. "Spelling Power: Focus on Spelling, Meaning, and Writing." *T.H.E. Journal* 28 (1): 64.

Snowball, Diane. 1996. "Spelling Strategies: How Kids Can Learn New Words for Their Writing." *Instructor* 106 (3): 37.

Websites

In a recent Internet check for spelling, 151,173 entries were cited focusing on spelling, high-frequency words, rules, and teaching strategies. Following are some helpful cites:

Burden, Peter. 2000. **WWlib–Notes on American English**. University of Worlverhapton. Accessed 4 April: *www.scit.wlv.ac.uk/~jphb/American.html*.

Carson-Dellosa. *www.carson.dellosa.com*. (word wall resources)

English Club.com. 2003. Accessed 4 April: *http://writing.englishclub.com/spelling_ible.htm*. (when to use *-ible* or *-able*)

Jones, Susan. 2000. **Spelling Differences Between American and British English.** Georgia State University. Accessed 4 April: *www.gsu.edu/~wwwesl/egw/jones /differences.htm*.

Lambert, Tony. **Spelling Rules.** Heber School District. Accessed 4 April: *www.heber .k12.ca.us/spellingrules.htm*.

Most often confused homophone list. 2003. Accessed 6 April: *www.Marlodge .supanet.com/wordlist/homophon.html*.

Works Cited

Bean, Wendy, and Chrys Bouffler. 1997. *Read, Write, Spell*. York, ME: Stenhouse.

Bear, Donald R., Marcia Invernizzi, Shane Templeton, and Francine Johnston. 2000. *Words Their Way: Word Study for Phonics, Vocabulary, and Spelling Instruction*. Upper Saddle River, NJ: Prentice Hall.

Beers, Kylene. 1998. "Choosing Not to Read: Understanding Why Some Middle Schoolers Just Say No." In *Into Focus: Understanding and Creating Middle School Readers*, ed. Kylene Beers and Barbara G. Samuels, 37–63. Norwood, MA: Christopher-Gordon.

Carlsen, G. Robert. 1974. "Literature Is." *English Journal* 63 (2): 23–27.

Carson-Dellosa. 2001. The Four Blocks Literacy Model Word Wall Plus for Upper Grades. Greensboro, NC: Carson-Dellosa.

Chomsky, Noam. 1957. *Syntactic Structures*. The Hague, Netherlands: Mouton.

Daniels, Harvey. 1994. *Literature Circles: Voice and Choice in the Student-Centered Classroom*. York, ME: Stenhouse.

Early, Margaret. 1960. "Stages of Growth in Literacy Appreciation." *English Journal* 49: 161–67.

Fitzsimmons, Robert J., and Bradley M. Loomer. 1977. *Spelling Research and Practice*. Iowa City: State Department of Public Instruction and The University of Iowa.

Fry, Edward, Jacqueline Kress, and Dona Lee Fountoukidis. 2000. *The Reading Teacher's Book of Lists*. 4th ed. Paramus, NJ: Prentice Hall.

Gates, Arthur I. 1931. "An Experimental Comparison of the Study-Test and Test-Study Methods of Spelling." *Journal of Educational Psychology* 22 (1): 7, 10–11.

Gentry, J. Richard. 1982. "GYNS AT WORK." *Reading Teacher* 36: 192–200.

———. 1987. *Spel . . . Is a Four-Letter Word*. Portsmouth, NH: Heinemann.

———. 1997. *My Kid Can't Spell! Understanding and Assisting Your Child's Literacy Development*. Portsmouth, NH: Heinemann.

Gentry, J. Richard, and Jean Wallace Gillet. 1993. *Teaching Kids to Spell.* Portsmouth, NH: Heinemann.

Goodman, Ken. 1993. *Phonics Phacts.* Portsmouth, NH: Heinemann.

Hanna, Paul R., et al. 1966. *Phoneme-Grapheme Correspondences as Cues to Spelling Improvement.* OE-32008. Washington, DC: U.S. Department of Health, Education, and Welfare.

Hawley, W. E., and J. Gallup. 1922. "The List Versus the Sentence Method of Teaching Spelling." *Journal of Educational Research* 5: 306–10.

Henderson, Edmund. 1980. "Word Knowledge and Reading Disability." In *Developmental and Cognitive Aspects of Learning to Spell: A Reflection of Word Knowledge,* by Edmund H. Henderson and James W. Beers, 138–48. Newark, DE: International Reading Association.

———. 1990. *Teaching Spelling.* Boston: Houghton Mifflin.

Henderson, Edmund H., and James W. Beers. 1980. *Developmental and Cognitive Aspects of Learning to Spell: A Reflection of Word Knowledge.* Newark, DE: International Reading Association.

Henderson, Edmund H., and Shane Templeton. 1986. "A Developmental Perspective of Formal Spelling Instruction Through Alphabet, Pattern, and Meaning." *The Elementary School Journal* 86 (5): 305–16.

Horn, Ernest. 1926. *A Basic Vocabulary of 10,000 Words Most Commonly Used in Writing.* Iowa City: College of Education, University of Iowa.

———. 1939. "The Validity and Reliability of Adult Vocabulary Lists." *The Elementary English Review* 16: 134.

Horn, T., and H. J. Otto. 1954. *Spelling Instruction: A Curriculum-Wide Approach.* Austin: Bureau of Laboratory School, University of Texas.

Hughes, Margaret, and Dennis Searle. 1997. *The Violent E and Other Tricky Sounds.* York: ME: Stenhouse.

Kelly, T. F. 1992. "Spelling: Tyranny of the Irrelevant." *The Effective School Report* (August): 3.

Laminack, Lester L., and Katie Wood. 1996. *Spelling in Use: Looking Closely at Spelling in Whole Language Classrooms.* Urbana, IL: National Council of Teachers of English.

Pinnell, Gay Su, and Irene Fountas. 1998. *Word Matters: Teaching Phonics and Spelling in the Reading/Writing Classroom.* Portsmouth, NH: Heinemann.

Reed, Charles. 1971. "Children's Perceptions of the Sounds of English: Phonology from Three to Six." *Harvard Educational Review* 41:1–34.

Richards, Jan. 2002. "Taking the Guesswork Out of Spelling." *Voices from the Middle* 9 (3): 16–18.

Shaughnessy, Mina P. 1977. *Errors and Expectations: A Guide for the Teacher of Basic Writing.* New York: Oxford University Press.

Sitton, Rebecca. 1995. *Spelling Sourcebook Series*. Spokane, WA: Egger.

Snowball, Diane, and Faye Bolton. 1999. *Spelling K–8: Planning and Teaching*. York, ME: Stenhouse.

Spradley, James. 1979. *The Ethnographic Researcher*. New York: Holt, Rinehart and Winston.

Strickland, James. 1997. *From Disk to Hard Copy*. Portsmouth, NH: Heinemann.

Templeton, Shane. 1979. "Spelling First, Sound Later: The Relationship Between Orthography and Higher Order Phonological Knowledge in Older Students." *Research in the Teaching of English* 13: 255–64.

———. 1983. "Using the Spelling/Meaning Connection to Develop Word Knowledge in Older Students." *Journal of Reading* 27: 8–14.

Thibodeau, Gail. 2002. "Spellbound: Commitment to Correctness." *Voices from the Middle* 9 (3): 19–22.

Trahan, Donald E., and Glenn J. Larrabee. 1983, 1988. Continuous Visual Memory Test. Odessa, FL: Psychological Assessment Resources.

Wilde, Sandra. 1996. "A Speller's Bill of Rights." *Primary Voices K–6* (November).

Zar, Jerrold H. 1994. "Candidate for a Pullet Surprise." *Journal of Irreproducible Results*. Cambridge, MA: Wisdom Simulators.

Index